"CLEARLY THE BEST"
A History of

Brewery, Aberbeeg

by Ray Morris

This book is dedicated to my dear mother
Mrs Floss Morris

Old Bakehouse Publications

Abertillery

First published in February 1997

ISBN 1 874538 46 8

Published in the U. K. by
Old Bakehouse Publications
Church Street,
Abertillery, Gwent NP3 lEA
Telephone: 01495 212600 Fax: 01495 216222

Made and printed in the UK
by J.R. Davies (Printers) Ltd.

Foreword by Brian o'C Blake

Sales Managing Director Bass Wales and West

In an industry undergoing massive change it is worthwhile, even if only occasionally, to pause and reflect on where we have come from and how we got here.

I am indebted to Ray Morris for providing me with just such an opportunity.

I was fortunate to spend two parts of my career in Aberbeeg, first between 1976 and 1978 when Welsh Brewers Ltd., reopened the offices as headquarters for Welsh Brewers East and subsequently between 1983 and 1989, when as the "last" Managing Director at Aberbeeg I was responsible for moving the operations to the Garden Festival Site at Ebbw Vale.

The later stages of Ray's work deals with my time in Aberbeeg and brings back many fond memories of my time there and the wonderful people with whom I worked, Dilwyn Jones, Dorothy Arndel, Eldred Probert and many others who feature in these pages.

By the time I arrived in Aberbeeg, brewing operations had transferred to Cardiff and the site had become our major distribution centre servicing the South Wales Valleys across to the English Border. It was beginning to show its age with erosion caused by the river (which flowed under the yard and offices) creating major structural problems These problems allied to the need to expand our operation led to the decision to seek a new site.

In order to ensure that we maintained contact with the community in which we had worked for over 150 years, I was commissioned by the Board of Bass Wales and West Ltd., to find a site to replace the Webbs site and that I was to "leave my car in Aberbeeg and walk" until I found a suitable replacement.

With the aid of the then M.P. for Blaenau Gwent the Rt. Hon. Michael Foot M.P. and the good offices of the Blaenau Gwent Council we were able to relocate our offices and depot together with our employees on the Garden Festival Site in Ebbw Vale.

So it was that over 150 years of connections between the brewing industry and the community of Aberbeeg was finally severed, not in collapse as had happened with the Mining and Railway Industries but out of a need to expand and modernise.

While everyone who moved to Ebbw Vale would agree that working conditions and accommodation are far superior in the new site, many of us still cherish the memories of the "old brewery".

Ray's work captures, in words and pictures the period between 1838 and 1990 but for Webbs and its successor Companies, 1990 was yet another landmark on the road to 2038.

Of one thing I am certain, with the quality of the people in the area, the heirs of the Webbs tradition will continue to thrive and I hope that there will be a Ray Morris around to record their achievements into the second half of the 21st Century.

Contents

Introduction

My personal interest in Webbs Brewery Ltd. at Aberbeeg began to develop during the 1960s when, with my father-in-law Mr. Percy Olding, we were often involved in general repair work for the company and the numerous public houses it administered. The Brewery and the Hanbury Hotel, both significant landmarks in the village were demolished in the Autumn of 1990, a sad day for many.

This event prompted me to consider producing a permanent record of the history of this once-renowned and respected brewer of fine ales. The research for this book absorbed many, many hours of work over a period of some 3 years and were it not for the dedicated assistance of my wife, the project would have been even longer on the 'drawing board'. Thank you Lynne for your help and encouragement.

Investigation and research through numerous sources revealed a host of interesting facts surrounding the formation of Webbs Brewery, dating back to the early years of the 19th century. Whilst over the years a little licensed legend may have found its way into the company history, the origins do appear to rest with three Webbs brothers who resided in the Staffordshire area. Each brother was said to have received the princely sum of £1000 from their apparently affluent parents, with which to formulate their own fame and fortune.

One was to develop early machines for grass-cutting, another formed the nationally acclaimed Webbs flower and vegetable seed company and the third was to establish a brewing business that was to last for almost 150 years. Also included with the historical data in this book is a wide collection of photographs. These photographs I hope will help re-kindle a few memories for everyone, not just those readers who may have worked at the Brewery at some time in their life. The book is also designed for those who can well remember just how Aberbeeg felt with its sweet aroma, sounds and sense of gratified importance in years gone by. Those days may seem distant to many but today's generation of Aberbeegians should still be proud of their memorable heritage.

Ray Morris

Chapter 1
Foundations of a Brewery

William Webb

William Webb was born on November 24th 1805 at eighteen minutes past five in the morning. He was baptized by his parents John and Dorothy at Tipton Staffordshire on December 22nd 1805. The Webb family left Staffordshire while William was an infant.

John went to work as a Land Agent for an eccentric Victorian writer and poet Walter Savage Landor on the Llanthony Abbey Estates.

Walter Savage Landor would not employ locals in any position of authority mainly because of the language barrier and his distrust of the Welsh.

During his time at Llanthony John had three bridges built over the River Honddu. On one of these bridges a few hundred yards north of the Abbey towards Capel-y-ffin, his name is carved into one of the stones.

Beer was brewed on the estate for shooting parties, and it is possible that the Webbs learned to make beer through this experience.

John Webb died in 1848, both John and Dorothy are buried in the Llanthony Churchyard.

Very little is known of William's childhood. However, on the 24th November 1825 in the Parish Church of Trevethin he married Harriet Walker.

The marriage certificate of William Webb and Harriet Walker.

Study of the certificate reveals that both Harriet and William signed their names in beautiful copperplate writing, proving that they were quite well educated.

Between 1826 and 1831 the Trevethin baptismal records show that William and Harriet had four children, three girls and one boy.

Between 1832 and 1839 there are no more entries of baptisms of Webbs children.

An extract from the baptismal records of Trevethin for 1831 the centre entry being William Henry.

On each of the entries in the register William's place of residence was the Varteg (near Blaenavon) and his occupation given as a rollturner.

It is possible that William worked in the Ironworks at Varteg. The Varteg Ironworks were established in 1803 by Knight and Company and later acquired by Kendricks and Company in 1826.

The Ironworks closed in 1864, the site of the works being close to the garage and filling station situated there nowadays.

Blaenavon Ironworks was a few miles north and the Golynos and Abersychan works a few miles south.

A rollturner was considered to be quite a skilled occupation also a dangerous one, being a two-man operation.

An old ironworks halfpenny depicting rollturners at work.

Between the late 1820s and the early 1830s William helped his father-in-law Mr Richard Walker to build a charcoal furnace at Abertillery. It was situated somewhere in the Cwmtillery valley.

There was a dispute around this time regarding the indiscriminate cutting of timber on land in the Cwmtillery valley belonging to Lord Abergavenny. The timber was used for charcoal.

A few years ago a Cwmtillery farmer whilst ploughing one of his fields found a cast iron ingot. He thought it might have been carried over the mountain from Blaenavon by mules, but it is more likely to have been an ingot cast at Cwmtillery.

By 1831 the Cwmtillery works produced small quantities of iron. A paper produced by The Monmouthshire Canal Company states.

Mr Richard Walker Cwmtillery Ironworks in 1831 produced 64 tons of iron; 1833 65 tons; 1835 1044 tons; 1837 266 tons; 1839-40 217 tons. Total Tonnage 1656 tons.

The Lake & Mountain. Cwmtillery. Mon. 081.

William's next venture was to enter into a partnership with a Mr Cadman and build a tinworks at Abertillery.

On June 18th 1839 William leased the Hanbury Arms Inn Aberbeeg from Mr David Phillips for a term of sixty-three years at a rent of £49 per annum. Included also was a parcel of land, a stableyard, a ball court and yard previously occupied by a Mr John Miles.

William also leased a dwelling house, brewhouse, malthouse and stables at Pont Aberbeeg suggesting that William Webb did not start the Aberbeeg Brewery or build the Hanbury Arms Inn.

Documents available also describe a tramroad on one side of the Brewery.

The tramroad described in an 1839 document would have started at Nantyglo Ironworks winding its way down past the Brewery to the wharf at Crumlin. The Nantyglo works were built in 1794 but by 1839 the owners were Joseph Bailey and his cousin Crawshay Bailey. Another tramroad came down the valley from Beaufort Ironworks, these works were developed in 1779 by John and Edward Kendall. The Beaufort works were bought by Joseph and Crawshay Bailey in 1833.

Another Ironworks at Ebbw Vale used the same tramroad, Homfrey, Cracroft and Watkins building the works in 1789, the company later passing into the ownership of Homfrey, Hartford and the Partridge Company.

The opening of the canals in the Eastern and Western Valleys certainly brought an influx of workers to the area. In 1801 the number of people in

9

the parish of Aberystruth was 820, but by the 1841 census the number had increased to 11272.

The man who William leased the Brewery and the Hanbury Inn from, Mr David Phillips, owned a great deal of land in and around Aberbeeg.

Mr Phillips' daughter Ann had married George Lawrence. The Lawrence's were a very influential family from Llantarnam, having two sons John and David, John achieving notable distinction in the iron and steel industry.

David Lawrence also had a very distinguished career, studying under Dr Jabez Thomas a well known Pontypool doctor.

David Lawrence's son Alfred Tristam became the most famous, he was born in Pontypool in 1843 and studied law at Trinity Hall Cambridge.

He was called to the Bar in 1866 and made Queen's Counsel in 1869. Knighted in 1904, he elevated to the bench as a Judge of the High Court on the 15th April 1921. Lord Alfred was raised to the Peerage in 1921 and took the title Lord Trevethin.

One of Lord Alfred's sons John became Baron Trevethin and Lord Oaksey the famous National Hunt Jockey. By 1839 William Webb had now found his niche in life and settled in Llanhilleth in a dwelling named Llanhilleth House. According to locals it was situated on the site now occupied by The Grace Pope Complex.

On September 2nd 1850 Harriet Webb passed away at the age of 44 years. She was buried in the Parish Church of St Iltyds, high on the mountain overlooking the Ebbw Valley.

Harriet Webb

The Aberbeeg census of 1851 shows William's household consisting of William Webb, a widower aged 46 Wine and Spirit Merchant. Daughters Elizabeth aged 24 and Dorothy aged 20. Son John Richard aged 15, Agnes aged 8 and Tom Alexander aged 4.

William had two servants Mary Thomas aged 15 of Aberbeeg and Mariah Perrett aged 20 from Cwmbran. Also in the house were two visitors William Wells, a Railway Clerk and Joan Price from Cwmyoy. He also employed five men at the Brewery.

Also shown on the 1851 census is the Hanbury Arms having as landlord, one William James, his wife Mary, a son James and a servant by the name of Elizabeth Wells. The population of Abersytruth had now risen by 3111 people since the 1841 census, the figure was now 14383.

Families came to industrial South Wales from all over the country for better wages in the ironworks and small levels. Also traders from the market towns of Brecon and Carmarthenshire came to sell their wares in these new lucrative areas. Some families were driven into South Wales trying to escape a life of poverty and despair.

The Irish came over in the 1850s to escape the potato famines. The author's Irish great grandmother was Margaret McHale from County Mayo who came over with her parents and made a new home for themselves in Risca.

The Monmouthshire Canal without a doubt was a great feat of engineering. But as early as 1845 a meeting was held at the Kings Head Hotel in Newport by the proprietors of the canal to remodel all existing tramroads to render them suitable for locomotion hauiage and to become sole carriers over those lines once it had been achieved.

This opened the way for more iron and minerals to be produced. It also signalled a decline in the use of traffic on the canal. The weather created a lot of problems for the owners of the canal, in hot summers and droughts, the water levels dropped despite Penyfan Pond being used as a feeder. While in severe winters, the canal froze causing chaos with stockpiles of iron at Crumlin Wharf.

In 1849 tenders were sent out by David Jones, company engineer for the Monmouthshire Railway and Canal Co. for booking offices and waiting rooms at Crumlin, Aberbeeg, Cwmtillery, Blaina and Ebbw Vale. Additional tenders were also invited for extra wagons for carrying pitwood, coke and other materials. The Aberbeeg sidings were built in 1849, each was a mile long and eight in number, 2000 tons of tramplates being used on 32000 larch sleepers.

On December 23rd 1850 the first passenger train made the journey from Newport to Blaina, a journey which took one and three quarter hours. The line to Ebbw Vale opened on April 19th 1852. The train parted

11

at Aberbeeg with one half going to Ebbw Vale and the other half continuing to Blaina.

The engine sheds and goods yard were built in 1858 on the lower side of Aberbeeg. A new shed was commissioned and built in 1919 where the Bawn Brothers Foundry stands today.

Before leaving the 1850s and all the activity in and around Aberbeeg, mention must be made of the viaduct at Crumlin. Construction began in May 1853 by Mr T W Kennard for the Newport, Abergavenny and Hereford Railway. On December 18th 1853 the first column was invested by Lady Isabella Fitzmaurice, wife of the Chairman of the Company. The iron bridge was 200 feet (61 metres) high, 1658 feet (505 metres) long and built at a cost of £62,000. It was opened on Whit Monday 1857 and witnessed by a crowd of 20000. The last passenger train ran on the bridge on 15th June 1964. A scene for the film 'Arabesque', with Gregory Peck and Sophia Loren was taken on the viaduct shortly before it was demolished in 1966.

By the next census of 1861 William Webb had remarried and in the Webb's house on census day we find William Webb aged 55 Maltster, Spirit and Wine Merchant. Ann, his wife aged 45, born Llandeilo, Agnes daughter, aged 19 born Aberbeeg and Tom Alexander aged 14 born Aberbeeg.

Two servants, Ann James aged 25 and John James aged 14 born Llandeilo were also included in the census.

The number of men employed at the Brewery was not given but with so much activity in and around Aberbeeg at this time, it is reasonable to assume that the Brewery would have employed a few more than the five men on the 1851 census.

William's daughter Elizabeth married a Mr John Crook and at one time they were landlords in the Hanbury. Mary Ann Dorothy, another daughter of William had also taken a husband, Mr Thomas H Bevan.

William Webb had made the brewing and malting business into two firms. The malting side he kept for himself and the brewing division he gave to his sons and sons-in-law. Both companies were situated at the rear of the Hanbury Arms.

The two companies then traded as William Webb Wine and Spirit Merchant and Webb Bros and Company.

In 1860 William was an active partner in an enterprise called Webb, Spittle and Partieh. Together they were responsible for the sinking of the Aberbeeg Colliery at a cost of £20,000. This company operated the colliery for about twelve years.

By 1876 Aberbeeg Colliery was owned by a Mr W Powell, its later owners were Powell & Sons. The Powells might well have been the same family who owned Penybont, Gray and Vivian Collieries and operated as Powell Tillery.

Budds and Company owned the colliery from around 1900 also owning a few levels in the Blackwood area. William's son William Henry died on 26th May 1866. He was born in Varteg in 1831, and helped his father at Aberbeeg, being described in one directory as a maltster.

Aberbeeg Colliery.

Gray Colliery Abertillery.

During his years at Aberbeeg William produced stone bottles to sell his Wines and Spirits in.

They were made at Bristol by a firm of potters named Price, the bottles held either one or two gallons of liquid. The letters cut in the bottles were William Webb Wine & Spirit Merchant Aberbeeg Nr Newport.

On December 4th 1872 William's second wife Ann died, she was fifty two years old and was also buried at St Iltyd's Church.

So once again William was a widower but not for long for at the age of 69 he married for the third time. The marriage took place at St Iltyd's Parish Church, Llanhilleth.

The marriage certificate of William Webb and Elizabeth Jones.

Mr R T Martin and his wife with John E Webb's children. Left to right are Kenneth Webb, Mr and Mrs Martin, Leslie Webb the infant with brothers and sister Martin, Douglas and Eileen.

1881 is the last census containing information about William; he still resided at Llanhilleth House and that census shows:

William Webb aged 75 Maltster Wine & Spirit Merchant. Elizabeth, wife aged 69 born at Howton Grove Herefordshire. Maria Williams aged 19 domestic born in Govilon. Minnie Rope aged 11 domestic born in Newport.

The census also stated that William employed eight men.

At an auction in 1881 William successfully bid for one of the leases from David Phillips, so now William owned the dwelling house, brewhouse and malthouse and the ground upon which they stood.

William Webb died on March 27th 1883 aged 77 years and a brief account of his life appeared in the Pontypool Free Press.

'We much regret to record the death of William Webb of Llanhilleth House which took place after a long and protracted illness on the 27th March in the 78th year of his life. The deceased gentleman was more particularly identified with his business as a Wine, Spirit and Maltster.

In 1830 he assisted the late Mr Richard Walker his father-in-law in the erection of a charcoal forge in Abertillery thence he went to the Varteg only to return to Abertillery where he went into a partnership with a Mr Cadman and erected a Tinworks. In 1860 he was an active partner in the firm of Webb, Spittle and Partieh who sunk Aberbeeg Pit which they ran for about twelve years.

*The ancient church of St Iltyd's with The Carpenter's Arms
public house close by.*

The founder William Webb in the later years of his long life.

16

In the foreground is William Webb's 'Llanhilleth House', since demolished and replaced by the Grace Pope Complex.

The information was probably given to the newspapers by J R Webb. Whilst some of the dates do not tie up with the author's research, in 1825 it is known that William was already living in the Varteg and up to 1831, busy starting his family. It has also been known that a Richard Walker did have an ironworks producing by 1831.

By these achievements it shows William Webb to have been a truly remarkable man. He would in his lifetime have seen Aberbeeg develop from a small hamlet when he first arrived, to a thriving and quite important village and railway junction by the time of his death.

Chapter 2

The Webb Brothers

John Richard Webb 1835-1908
Tom Alexander Webb 1846-1892

John Richard was born on July 16th 1835 in Aberbeeg. He was 45 years old when William died and was educated at the Kemp School, Long Ashton, Bristol.

He returned to Aberbeeg after his schooling and helped his father in his businesses. He married Eleanor Susannah Davies, the daughter of George and Susannah Davies. Eleanor was born in Blaina on July 6th 1843, her father being a landlord of one of the pubs in the Blaina/Nantyglo area.

It is interesting just how John and Eleanor met, perhaps John visited the Blaina pub with his father, or maybe George and Eleanor had cause to visit the Aberbeeg Brewery. It certainly suggests that Webbs were selling beer in the Blaina/Nantyglo area in the 1850s/1860s.

During the early years of their marriage John and his wife had their fair share of sorrow. In these Victorian times child mortality was high and two of their children George William and Jesse died in infancy.

John Richard Webb

Tom Alexander Webb was also born in Aberbeeg, on 5th July 1846. He was educated at Wesleyan College in Taunton. After his education was complete he also returned to Aberbeeg to help his father and brother in the business. In 1865 Tom with the consent of the other partners was also made a partner in the firm of Webb Brothers and Company.

Brondeg House built for J R Webb and family, later used by Managing Directors.

In 1871 the census shows Tom living in Brondeg house at Aberbeeg with his brother Richard and family.

John R Webb aged 36. Brewer and maltster born Aberbeeg. Eleanor aged 27, wife born in Blaina. John Edgar aged 4 son born in Aberbeeg. Harriet aged 2 daughter born in Aberbeeg. Tom A Webb aged 25 brother, brewer born in Aberbeeg. Emily Davies aged 14 sister-in-law born in Blaina.

The Hanbury Arms was now occupied by Lewis Lewis aged 32 and his wife Mary aged 26 and a one year old daughter Elizabeth. Their servants were Elizabeth Brocoi, Sarah James and Phoebe Weobly.

On February 14th 1877 Tom Alexander Webb married Agnes Emily Davies at the church of St Illtyd's Llanhilleth. Agnes Emily was the sister of Eleanor Webb nee Davies.

By 1881 Tom and Agnes Emily had started a family in Aberbeeg, Gladys aged 3 and Florence aged 1 who were both born in the village.

The marriage certificate of Tom Alexander Webb and Agnes Emily Davies.

His brother John is listed as John R Webb aged 46 Wine and Spirit Merchant. Eleanor wife aged 37 employing a cook named Emma Cox aged 22 born at Ebbw Vale and Mary Hatton aged 24 a domestic servant who was born in the Forest of Dean.

Eleven men were now employed by J R, four of these are to be found on the census at Aberbeeg. Joseph Clarke aged 44 a cellarman, Benjamin Evans aged 38 a brewery haulier, Thomas Jenkins aged 40 a brewery labourer. All three lived in Woodland Terrace and the fourth was William Bobbett aged 38 living at Crooks Row.

The census for the parish of Aberystruth was 18672 persons.

In May 1882 William Webb's daughter Elizabeth Crook died aged 55 and in the August of 1882 her husband John died at the age of 57, John Crook was a partner in the Webb Bros Company.

William Webb left his Wine and Spirit Company (sometimes called The Malting Firm) and the grounds and buildings on which the brewery and malthouse stood, to John Richard and Tom Alexander Webb. They produced their own stone bottles, the logo inscribed on them was as follows:

JR Webb & TA Webb Wine & Spirit Merchant Aberbeeg nr Newport.

Besides owning the Malting Firm and being partners in the Webbs Bros Co, the two brothers, like their father started to buy large amounts of land and property around the area. These were known as The Abertillery and Cwm Estates. In 1886 Tom A Webb and his family left Aberbeeg to reside in Waun Wern House on the Crumlin Road near Pontypool. The house at one time belonged to Dr David Lawrence mentioned in Chapter One.

Waun Wern House was demolished a long time ago and was situated where the Waun Wern Caravan Park now stands. In March 1892 after a long illness, Tom A Webb died when he was 45 years old, he left three girls and one boy.

Tom Webb is buried at St Illtyd's near his parents, the service was conducted by the curate of the Tranch Church Pontypool.

His widow Agnes Emily married some years later a Parson Phillips-Davies and they moved to the village of Hollington near St Leonards on Sea.

John R Webb also had his share of sorrow, his wife Eleanor died on May 29th 1881 she was 38 years old. After the death of their first two children, they had four more who survived, John Edgar; Harriet Annie; Alice Ellen and Kate.

By 1891 John R had remarried and he was living in his father's Llanhilleth House. The 1891 census stated John R Webb aged 56 Wine & Spirit Merchant. Clara L wife aged 37 born in Bath Somerset. John E son aged 23 single born in Aberbeeg. Kate daughter aged 18 single born in Aberbeeg.

Between 1890 and 1900 most of the deep mines were sunk, some a little earlier than this. The closest to Aberbeeg was the Arael Griffin sunk by John Lancaster in 1891.

The Waunlwyd Ebbw Vale Iron Coal Co 1876.

The Marine Colliery sunk by the Ebbw Vale Iron & Coal 1889.

The Vivian Colliery sunk by Powell Bros 1889.

Cwmtillery sunk by South Wales Coal Co. 1860.

The Gray Colliery sunk by Powell Bros 1884.

John R Webb and his wife Clara while on holiday at Aberystwyth.

21

These collieries brought in a floodtide of migrant workers all hoping for regular work with better wages. The census for the area at this time was approximately 20000 people.

Between 1890 and 1900 the Griffiths Bros. Brewery in Blaina opened, the Chivers & Sons Brewery started in Cwmtillery and the Western Valley Brewery at Crumlin. All these were in direct competition to Webbs Brewery. The Western Valley Brewery at Crumlin was situated near the Viaduct Inn, a pub still open to this day. This brewery was taken over in 1900 by D F Pritchard. Francis Pritchard was a former manager of the Andrew Buchan Brewery at Rhymney. The Buchan Brewery was built by the Rhymney Iron Co in 1836, therefore Francis Pritchard was well qualified to be a brewer. He also bought Crumlin Hall, the house once occupied by Mr Kennard the designer and builder of Crumlin Viaduct.

Francis Pritchard brewed some fine ales and stouts. He increased the size of his company in 1916 by taking over the Christmas Evans Brewery at Heolygerrig Merthyr. After the takeover he closed the brewery but retained the public houses.

During his time at Crumlin 1900-1930 he produced a great quantity of stone bottles. Incidentally most bottle collectors will probably have one of the Francis Pritchard stone bottles in their collection.

The Chivers Brewery was situated on Crook Hill in Cwmtillery, it was a small brewery with not much space for expansion. Mr Alfred Chivers and later Joseph Chivers and sons were the proprietors. They owned two pubs The White Horse Inn and The Fountain both in Penybont. The Chivers family tried on several occasions to obtain a licence to sell beer to the public direct from the brewery but each time they applied to the magistrates for permission, Webbs solicitor Mr Brasseur objected and Chivers were refused. It is not certain when brewing ceased, but the brewery was still standing in 1970. There was a tunnel from the brewery leading down to the Fountain Inn and when the brewery closed, quite a number of Chivers stone bottles were found in it.

Webbs Bros and Company produced a number of brass tokens about 38mm in size. One side of the token showed Webbs Bros & Co Aberbeeg and the reverse side Barm Penny, they also produced three pences, one shilling and two shillings. The barm tokens were obtained by the public from the Brewery and could be exchanged for the barm, being the yeast taken from the top of the beer during the brewing process.

According to one local history book 'Mid Valley Nostalgia' by W W Tasker, a Mr Jeanes of Argoed Village provided a service to the village. He walked from Argoed to Penyfan Pond making his way down to Aberbeeg to purchase the barm with his tokens.

An early stone beer bottle   *Chivers Brewery*

The by-product of the brewing process was used to make bread or a home brew. Mr Jeanes carried the barm back to Argoed in two large jacks, then selling them at one penny a cup for drinking and three pence a basin for breadmaking.

Webbs were not alone in selling the waste barm. Yeast tokens for other breweries have turned up, but it does show how Webb Bros Company made money out of a waste product.

In May 1894 John R Webb was looked up to by the local people as a squire, almost a father figure.

A local gentleman, Mr John Thomas lived in a house called Twyn Goch, leaving all his worldly goods to his daughters Margaret and Jane in his will as witnessed by J R Webb and H Price, Clerk of Aberbeeg. Following their father's death in 1908, the ladies continued to live at Twyn Goch making their living by selling garden produce grown themselves, particularly fruit. Margaret became known locally as 'Maggie Gooseberry' and the lane at the side of Twyn Goch was called Maggie's Lane. This lane was originally part of the old parish track called Rhiw Goch. The house changed hands in 1941 and is in fact now occupied by the author and his wife, the house name also having changed to Bryn Goch.

A three pence Webb's barm token.

In 1902 the Collings family moved into the Hanbury Arms and the Hotel was run by members of this same family until the 1970s. It was Annie Collings first, then her son Howard and his wife, followed by Howard's wife for the final years.

Aberbeeg as it appeared in 1904.

The Intermediate School at Abertillery which was demolished in the 1980s. Originally opened in 1897 it was built on a plot of land given to the community by the Webb Brothers John Richard and Tom Alexander.

In the summer of 1904 a court case began in London. The case concerned the Bevans and the Webbs. This was the fourth case in fourteen years and it ended years of family fighting, which involved uncles, nephews and nieces. William had two businesses, The Malting & Spirit Co. and a subsidiary business The Brewery Co. In 1856 he made his son-in-law John Crook a partner in the Brewery Company. John Crook had married William's daughter Elizabeth and they were at one time landlords at the Hanbury Hotel.

Thomas Anthony Bevan was another partner, he having married William's daughter, May Ann Dorothy.

The sons of William Webb were also made partners in the Brewery Co. His eldest son William Henry was first but he died at an early age in 1866. John Richard Webb was another partner and in 1865, the youngest son Tom Alexander Webb was made a partner, with the consent of the other associates.

William Webb then concentrated on the Malting & Spirits while the partners in the Brewery, which was now called Webbs Brother & Company developed the brewing. William Webb died in 1883 and left his Malting & Spirit Co to his two sons John Richard and Tom

Alexander. He also left them the first parcel of land that he had leased from David Phillips in 1839. This consisted of the Brewery Malthouse, a house and the stables. This Lease had been acquired by William Webb at an auction in 1881. The two brothers now owned the Malting firms, the land on which the Brewery stood and were also partners in Webbs Bros & Co. The Webbs Bros bought and supplied local pubs and the Malting and Spirit did the same, but if the Malting Co acquired new orders for the supply of Webbs beer, they charged the Webbs Bros Co a commission for obtaining the new order. The Webb Bros Co also charged the Malting & Spirit Co a percentage for selling spirits in the Webb Bros pubs. The two brothers J R and T A Webb owned the malting firm and were partners in the Webb Bros firm, thus in a happy 'no lose' situation. The Malting and Spirit Co also charged the Webbs Bros annual rent for the parcel of ground the brewery stood on.

In November 1892 the second David Phillips lease, which involved the Hanbury Arms came onto the market and The Malting & Spirit Co bought it. The family dispute widened over this second purchase. The Webbs Bros claiming it had been purchased from under their noses, with the Malting & Spirit Co claiming the Webb Bros Co knew about the sale, but did not have capital available to buy the second lease. These were the main ingredients of the dispute, the first case coming to court in 1890. 1904 was the last case, the families involved were for the defence, John Richard Webb, John Edgar Webb, Mrs Emily Agnes Phillips Davies and Mr Henry Le Brasseur who represented Mr William Reginald Valentine Webb. The plaintiffs were The Reverend William Bevan, Mr Henry Crook Bevan a surgeon from Blaina, Mr Thomas Webb Bevan a surgeon from Nantyglo and Mrs Harriet Agnes Robinson a widow from Cardiff. They were all children of Mr Thomas A Bevan and Mary Ann Dorothy Bevan nee Webb.

At a meeting held on Wednesday July 26th 1905 the directors of J R & T A Webb Ltd passed a resolution that a draft agreement between The Rev William Bevan, Mr Henry Crook Bevan, Tom Webb Bevan and Mrs Harriet Agnes Robinson of the first part. Mr John Richard Webb, John Edgar Webb, Mrs Agnes E Phillips Davies and Mr Henry Le Brasseur of the second part and J R & T A Webb Co of the third part, providing for a consideration payable to the Bevan family for their share of the firm Webb Bros & Co.

A draft agreement was made between J R Webb, John E Webb, Mrs Agnes E Phillips Davies, Mr J Le Brasseur of the first part William Reginald Valentine Webb of the second part and J R & T A Webb Ltd of the third part.

For the purchase of the shares of the Webbs Family in the business of Webbs Bros & Co and the same was hereby approved and that an agreement be approved.

That all necessary arrangement to be made in order to amalgamate the business of Webbs Bros & Co with that of JR & TA Webb Ltd as from 1st October 1905. That all necessary steps be taken to alter the name of the company to Webbs Aberbeeg Ltd and to increase the capital of the company to £150,000 the resolution was passed.

250 Debentures in the company of £100 pounds each to be allotted as follows John Richard Webb of Brondeg House 200 Debentures number 111 to 310 inclusive for the total sum of twenty thousand pounds.

To Mr William Reginald Valentine Webb of Elgin Tower, Minehead, Somerset 50 Debentures number 311 to 360 at a total sum of five thousand pounds.

Mrs Agnes Emily Phillips Davies was the widow of Tom Alexander Webb and William Reginald Valentine Webb was the son of Tom Alexander Webb. He was known to the family as Reggie and he died in the 1920s following a diving accident. He dived into water that was too shallow and struck his head on a rock, the accident occurring while he was touring the United States.

Also, in September 1905, the firm of J R & T A Webb Wine and Spirit Merchants paid the Bevan family a considerable sum for their share of Webbs Brothers and Company.

The way was now open for the brewery to expand after years of family quarrels, the Malting Firm and Webbs Bros became Webbs Aberbeeg Ltd.

During late 1905 plans were drawn up for alterations and work started in 1906, the brewhouse was enlarged and barrellage increased.

New one and two-gallon stone bottles were produced, made by Hunts of Liverpool inscribed Webbs (Aberbeeg) Ltd Brewers Wine and Spirit Merchants Aberbeeg.

It is quite remarkable that John Richard attended his last meeting on 30th December 1907, although towards the end of his life the meetings took place at Brondeg House and not the brewery offices.

A newspaper report from January 1908 is reproduced below.

'On Friday evening, Mr John Richard Webb, of Brondeg House, Aberbeeg passed away after a long and painful illness, and by his death the district has lost one of its oldest inhabitants and one who has been intimately associated with its development. The deceased was head of the firm of 'Webbs Limited', Aberbeeg, who besides owning and carrying on the well-known brewery, also are the freeholders of the Cwm and Abertillery Estate.

An early picture of Cwm near Ebbw Vale showing the Victoria Hotel. This was one of the licensed premises which The Malting Company shared a commision arrangement with the Webbs Bros. Company.

John Richard Webb who died on January 10th 1908.

28

The deceased, who was born on July 16th, 1855, was the elder son of the late Mr William Webb of Aberbeeg, who was the founder of the brewery business and was also associated in the starting of the Abertillery Tinworks, the colliery at Aberbeeg now worked by Messrs Budd and several other coal levels and quarries in the district. The deceased was educated at the Kemp School, Long Ashton, Bristol and after leaving school he at once took an active share in his father's business for the building up of which he was largely responsible. The deceased with his brother, the late Mr T A Webb, gave the site for the Abertillery County Intermediate School, of which he was a life foundation governor. Up to three years ago the deceased was actively engaged in the supervision of the affairs of 'Webbs Limited', but since then he has not been able to take the same personal share in its management owing to a long and trying illness, which he bore with great fortitude and patience. He was attended throughout his illness by Dr J D Sullivan of Aberbeeg. Mr Webb was a staunch and loyal member of the Anglican Church, but he took no prominent part in political or other public affairs. The deceased was married twice, and by his first wife who died about 27 years ago he had four children: - Mr John Edgar Webb, Managing Director of 'Webbs Limited'; Mrs J Jefferies, of Warm Turn; Mrs S J Rawlings 'The Firs', Aberbeeg; and Miss Webb who lived with her father at Brondeg, Aberbeeg. The funeral which was of a private character took place yesterday (Thursday) at noon at Llanhilleth Churchyard.

THE FUNERAL

The funeral took place on the Thursday with interment in the family vault at St Illtyd's churchyard. It was a private service but signs of mourning were apparent everywhere. The cortege was headed by the Rector, the Reverend D Felix and Dr J D O'Sullivan followed by office staff and workers connected with the brewery.

Then came the coffin. The remains were enclosed in lead with an outer case of full panelled English oak with massive brass mountings. The inscription read:

John Richard Webb of Aberbeeg
Born July 16th 1835 : Died January 10th 1908

The coffin was conveyed in an open Victorian carriage drawn by four horses.

Many local shopkeepers closed their premises as a mark of respect as the procession made its way from Brondeg through the square and up to the old edifice high on the mountain top.

Among the mourners were J E Webb, son; J Jeffries, son-in-law; nephews, W R V Webb, W Lewis and Dr Donnellan, R Hanhan, R T Martin, Newport; D S Davies, Abersychan; H Le Brasseur, family solicitor;

E G Cooper, chief clerk; T Vachell, agent for Cwm and Abertillery Estates; W Stewart, Abertillery; J Stanfield, Llanhilleth; TM Evans, Newport and T J Yendall of Ebbw Vale.

Services were conducted at the residence, in the church and at the graveside by Reverend D Felix.

Wreaths were sent by Mrs J R Webb, widow; Miss Webb, Brondeg; Mr J E Webb, Nantyglo; the Nantyglo grandchildren; Mr & Mrs J Jeffries; Mr & Mrs F J Rawlings; Mr & Mrs W R V Webb; Mr & Mrs W Lewis; Dr & Mrs Donnellan; Mr Royd Hanhan; Mr T Martin; Mr D S Davies and Miss Davies, Abersychan; Misses Emily and P Davies, St Leonards on Sea; Mr & Mrs Cogswell, Bristol; Mrs J G Perry, Newport; Misses Emma and Ellen Hanhan; Miss Seabourne, London; Mr & Mrs Ridgeway; Mrs D Lewis; Miss Winifred Yendall; The office staff; Mr A Evans, Newport; Mr & Mrs Beessell, Clifton; The servants at Brondeg; Mr & Mrs T Evans, Newport; Mr & Mrs E G Cooper, Aberbeeg; Mr W Tossell, Cwm; Mrs Walters & Family, Newport; Workmen of the Brewery; Mr & Mrs T Yendall, Ebbw Vale; Messrs H & S Jones & Family, Abertillery; Mr & Mrs J Stanfield, Llanhilleth; Mr & Mrs J F Hawkins, Reading.

In 1908 the local shopkeepers would have been :-

Ebenezer Edmunds. Grocer, Draper and Baker. Agent for W A Gilbey Wine & Spirits

Annie Collings. Hanbury Hotel, Aberbeeg

Anna Clark. Grocer and Beer Retailer

George Cook. Grocer

Thomas Edmunds. Grocer and Ale and Porter Merchant

William Lewis. Shopkeeper

John Edward Rowland. Ironmonger

Herbert Twizzel. Hairdresser. Emma Twizzel, China

John Purchase. Boot Repairer

Henry Kibby. Provision Dealer

Lionel Thomas. The Emporium, Grocer, Baker

Of the above list it was Henry Kibby and his family who became the most well known in Aberbeeg and the surrounding area.

The Kibby's came to Aberbeeg from Bridgwater, Somerset. Henry was a miller and he operated from Glandwr.

Henry's son Harry opened his first shop 'The Stores' at Aberbeeg. This was situated where the Flyover Garage is today, Harry also ran a bakery on the same premises.

He had two horses for his deliveries to the community, delivering to Aberbeeg, Trinant and Manmoel in the early days. The horses were kept at Christchurch in fields where there are bungalows at the present time. Harry Kibby Junior can just remember one of his first jobs which was to catch the horses and bring them down to the Stores for his father.

After Harry Kibby Senior passed away his sons Arthur, Harry and John took over the family business. It was during these years that the Kibby empire expanded, particularly due to the efforts of the eldest son, Arthur. By the 1960s the Kibby Bros had acquired the shop opposite the Hanbury Hotel once owned by Courtney Edmunds.

They also had shops at

1 Railway Street, Llanhilleth	69 Meadow Street, Llanhilleth
Somerset Street, Abertillery	High Street, Brynmawr
Bethcar Street, Ebbw Vale	Trinant
Cross Street, Caerleon	Swffryd
Ty Isaf, Risca	Bridge Street, Cwm
High Street, Beaufort	

Harry Kibby on the right receives a bulk delivery of some well known baked beans.

In 1962 Unigate bought Kibbys and although it was then part of the Unigate Group they still traded under the Kibby name.

In the early '60s supermarkets became the modern way of shopping and the Unigate Group opened stores under the Kibby name in Abertillery, Brynmawr, Pontypool, Newport, Cardiff, Penarth, Taunton, Bristol and Cornwall.

When the Kibby brothers left Aberbeeg, the youngest son John purchased a Post Office in Torquay. Having sold the bungalow which he had built at the bottom of the Rhiw leading to Brynithel.

Arthur Kibby lived at Hillcrest, Christchurch, Aberbeeg now occupied by Mr T Sharrem and family. He left Aberbeeg and lived in the Chepstow area, and worked in Yate as a General Manager for Gardiners part of the Unigate Group.

Harry Kibby, the middle son lived in Kinra, Christchurch a bungalow built by local builder Mr Percy Olding and now occupied by Martyn and Debbie Butler and their family. Harry took up the position of Area Manager for Unigate South West, eventually moving to Paignton where he still lives today. He is the last of the Kibby brothers, Arthur and John are both deceased.

Bryn Goch House known as 'Maggie Gooseberry's cottage near old Rhiw Goch Track also known as Maggies Lane pictured in 1940.

An early photograph taken at the Brewery in 1892.

Lionel Thomas and members of his staff outside The Emporium, Aberbeeg.

Chapter 3
John Edgar Webb 1866-1918

John Edgar Webb and Margaret Annie Webb (nee Martin) with infant Kenneth Webb in 1894.

John Edgar was born in Aberbeeg in 1866 and was 42 years old when his father died. In the 1891 census he is shown as living in Llanhilleth House with his father and stepmother, his occupation described as a solicitor.

By June of the following year he had married Margaret Annie Martin of Newport, Margaret Annie being the daughter of Mr and Mrs R T Martin.

Mr Robert Thomas Martin was a very interesting character. He came to Newport in 1862 and was appointed assistant cashier with Thomas Powell & Sons who were colliery proprietors. Thomas Powell was operating small levels in Llanhilleth at one time, later moving to the Aberdare Valleys and sinking collieries there.

Powell and his wife went on an ill-fated hunting trip to Ethiopia, the party being butchered by natives. Henry Powell left for Ethiopia on hearing the news and brought back the bodies.

Thomas Powell was interred in the churchyard at Bassaleg. Powells Collieries were sold to Mr George Elliot and Partners and the Powell Duffryn Coal Co was formed. Mr Martin worked for Powell Duffryn for fifty years, operating the Newport offices. He was also a director and one time Chairman of Webbs Aberbeeg Limited.

John Edgar Webb and his wife moved into Llanhilleth House after they married. Later in 1898 after visiting Anglesey on a fishing trip, he was so impressed with the island that he returned in 1902 and built a new house there. It was situated at Rhosneigr overlooking the sea in a prime position. Meanwhile at Aberbeeg in 1898, negotiations had started between Monmouthshire County Council and Pontypool Park Estate to lease a parcel of land on which to build a police station.

The following year, the council accepted a tender by Charles Morgan and Evan Phillips both of Newbridge. The terms of the contract were that the police station would be built for the sum of £930 and it would be finished within sixteen weeks. A £5 per week penalty would be enforced if the contract went over the stipulated time, unless of course extras were added to the contract. When the police station was finished the final figure was £1011 excluding any wallpaper.

The following year a new post office was built adjacent to the police station.

The post office built in 1899 was not the first one, on the 1881 map a post office is shown by the Hanbury Arms Hotel.

The Red House Anglesey built for J Edgar Webb.

35

Marine Colliery, Cwm

Aberbeeg had a post office as early as the 1860s, a Martha Williams was in charge, letters arrived at 8.30am in the morning and were despatched at 4.40pm in the evening. By the late 1870s a Mr Thomas Jones and his family were in the post office. Descendants of the Jones family have suggested that William Webb invited Thomas Jones down from Herefordshire to work in the brewery as maltster and also operate the post office. The 1881 census shows

Thomas Jones aged 40 Maltster born Welsh Newton. Emma wife aged 56 born St Weonards. Sarah J aged 18 Postmistress born St Weonards. Edith G aged 12 born Cwmcarvon. Edith G aged 6 granddaughter born Cwmcarvon. Edward Ballinger aged 28 Maltster born Cwmcarvon.

It is also possible the Jones family might have been related to William Webb's third wife Elizabeth Jones. She was from the Skenfrith/Ross area quite near the above villages and Elizabeth Webb nee Jones' father, was also a Thomas Jones.

The post office at the turn of the century was occupied by Mr David Jenkins who had married one of the Jones family. In 1934 his son Clifford became Postmaster and held this post until 1975.

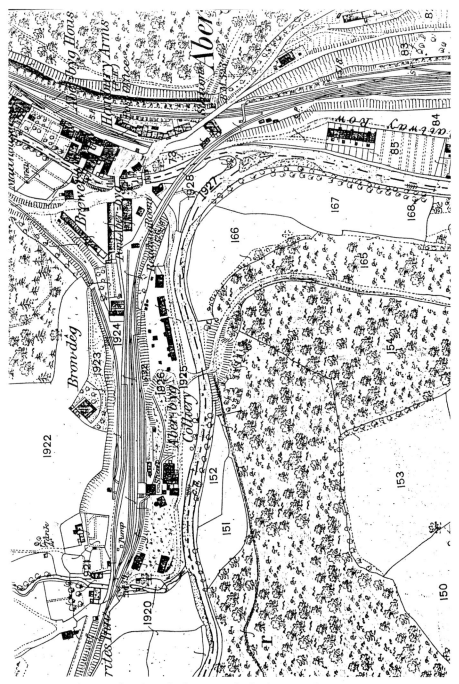

A map showing the lay-out of Aberbeeg in the year 1881.

The wedding photograph of John Edgar Webb and Margaret Annie Martin.

At the time of his father's death John Edgar and his family were living at Nantyglo in Hafodafol House. The children were William Edgar Kenneth; Martin Hugh; Margaret Eleanor Eileen; John Leslie Symons and the youngest George Douglas.

John Edgar was a member of the Anglican Church, he donating a lovely organ to St Michaels Church in Abertillery. Another church in the area at one time was offered a donation by Webbs but the rector refused to accept, as the money was obtained by ill-gotten gains (the sale of beer). By 1910 J Edgar left Nantyglo for Chepstow, to a new home named Larkfield House.

Larkfield House and grounds must have been very impressive, it included a farm, a herd of Jersey cows and seven gardeners who were employed to tend the lovely grounds. J Edgar also had a seven-mile stretch of the River Wye to fulfil his favourite hobby, fly fishing.

J Edgar was chauffeured to the brewery by one of the locals, a Mr Harries of Mathern. Harries died in action in France towards the end of World War One.

While researching old newspapers during the time of John Edgar Webb's management of the brewery, the author came across two interesting stories.

Larkfield from the air in the early 1950s.

From the South Wales Argus in 1910.

Run over by a Dray

An unfortunate accident which terminated in a fatal occurrence on Friday 21st at Aberbeeg. William Blakeley who resides at 3 Brewery Terrace Aberbeeg was employed as a haulier by Messrs Webbs Aberbeeg, while proceeding along the road near Arrow sidings, Abertillery he fell from his dray and was run over. He received injuries of a serious nature and was removed to the County Hospital Newport where he succumbed on Monday.

The Inquest

The inquest was held at the Newport Town Hall on Wednesday by Mr Lyndon Moore.

Emily Kate Blakeley said her husband was in the employ of Messrs Webbs Ltd, Aberbeeg, and he went out to work about 8.30am on Friday morning. He was in good health and was brought home again about 5.30pm by some men, he was suffering from injuries received through falling off the dray that he was driving on Blaina Road. Dr Sullivan came to attend him and he was ordered to the Newport Hospital where he later died.

Eric Lang, surgeon said at the post mortem, he found a rupture of the bowels in two places and general peritonitis which caused his death. Hubert Robert

Turner, goods guard at Aberbeeg, deposed to being in the Arrow sidings when he saw a dray coming along the road when the dray was opposite him, the deceased fell off, the horses bolted and were found near Abertillery. Charles Workman brakesman at Aberbeeg said Turner called his attention to the deceased, Mr Blakeley who was leaning against the railings at the side of the road. Mr Workman attempted to render first aid but the deceased would not let him. When the horses were brought back, Mr Blakeley said he would drive them back to the brewery even though the dray had passed over his stomach.

Alfred Edward Bowen brewer said he heard of the accident and went on his bicycle to investigate. Mr Blakeley told him the horses shied and he fell off the dray. The dray, which was loaded at the time had passed over his stomach. The jury returned a verdict of death caused by injuries received through the accident.

The Central Hotel, Llanhilleth.

Another case in the South Wales Argus.

Central Hotel, Llanhilleth - Saturday 1st July 1911.
Important action affecting the licensing trade came before Mr Justice Lawrence and a special jury at the Monmouthshire Assizes on Tuesday afternoon. It was an action by Mr Telford Evans, Cardiff, as the lessor of the Central Hotel at Llanhilleth, one of the largest and most modern houses in the Western Valleys. There was a counter claim for £100 in respect of alleged breaches of covenant. Mr

40

A Powell K C and Mr Geoffrey Lawrence appeared for Mr Telford Evans and Mr Vachell K C and Mr A J Davies K C and Mr S T John Micklewaithe appeared for Mr Albert Simmonds. Mr Powell in his opening statement said the action was to recover possession from the lessor of the premises known as The Central Hotel at Llanhilleth. It was erected several years ago by Mr Telford Evans architect and surveyor Cardiff to meet the needs of an important mining centre. After a lapse of five years the justices licensed the premises. The cost of the building was £6,000. The lease between Mr Evans and Mr Simmonds was entered into on the 1st March 1909 and was to run for 7 years at £2,000 premium to be paid and £400 per annum as rent.

From March 1909 to 1911 Mr Evans complained of the way Mr Simmonds ran the Central. Although it was a free house, most of the beer came from Webbs at Aberbeeg. A statement from the barmaid Annie Powell said that when a customer asked for a pint of Bass she was told to serve them Webbs. Caroline Coles another barmaid at the Central also stated that when customers complained about the beer being Webbs she just took it back and replaced it with a Webbs pint from a different pump.

Mr Evans also complained about the clientele eg. women of a loose character.

Mr Telford Evans in the witness box told of a visit in the early part of 1910 in the company of two other gentlemen. When he proceeded to the smoke room they saw a man asleep in a drunken condition on the sofa. The man's wife was also in a drunken condition and was behaving in a disgraceful manner with another man.

Annie Powell in her testimony stated that during the time she worked at the Central, about nine months, she had seen immoral women about the premises. They were allowed to stay as long as they liked. This witness thought Mr Simmonds knew about it, because she had told him about it. The charwoman aged about 50 years was allowed to stay at the Hotel for all hours and Annie Powell had seen her take money from men and go outside with them. Another woman would accept money and invite men into her house. Gladys Hill another barmaid said that as far as the women who frequented the Hotel were concerned, she had seen them remain behind after work, follow men into the lavatory and return a short time later.

Another witness Herbert John Stone stated he could not say anything as to the management of the Hotel, although he had spoken to Mr Simmonds about the women frequenting the premises.

Mr Vachell said Mr Simmonds had done everything in his power to conduct the house properly. There had been a lot of talk about immoral women. When Stone was asked whether he had seen anything immoral at Llanhilleth he said not to his knowledge.

Mr Arthur Withers, an engineer of 16 Raglan Road, Hengoed said he used to live in Llanhilleth and some of the women who frequented the Central Hotel were not of good character. His wife complained about it to him and she ceased to visit the Hotel.

Mr Simmonds the defendant in the witness box said he was the occupier of the Central Hotel. In December 1908 he had a brother employed by Webbs Brothers Aberbeeg Brewery, his brother's occupation was a traveller. His brother had spoken to him about the Central Hotel and as a result he went to Cardiff to see Mr Evans and following five or six interviews an agreement was drawn up. Mr Simmonds agreed to supply electrical fittings and some bar fittings, pumps etc. Mr Simmonds stated that he employed six girls and two men. He considered he had sufficient staff for conducting the business of his house. Mr Simmonds also stated that his family had done business with Webbs for 40 years. He made no contract with them for the supply of beer and he was free to order with any firm.

The Counsel for Mr Simmonds then showed invoices for the last two years' trading, showing Simmonds had bought 703 barrels of beer from other breweries.

During cross examination by Mr Powell, Simmonds admitted that he had borrowed £3,000 from Webbs and they were anxious to enter into an agreement with him. But he had informed them that he could not, as the terms of the lease would not allow him to do so. Mr Le Brasseur a Newport solicitor and Webbs director stated that he was quite familiar with negotiations with Mr Evans the hotel owner, and he denied anything suggesting a tie between Mr Simmonds and Webbs.

Mr Bishop solicitor for the defendant stated there was absolutely no arrangement whereby the defendant would take a certain quantity of beer from Webbs. They naturally expected that their loan of £3,000 would mean that they would obtain a good proportion of the defendant's trade. Alderman T J Parry a county valuer examined the fittings Mr Simmonds had provided at the Hotel and he found them to be in order. He also stated Webbs beers had a good reputation in the valleys and he was struck with the low price Simmonds was paying for it. If it had been a tied house it would have been 10 shillings more a barrel.

The judge in his summing up observed that the action brought by the plaintiff was based on two grounds. First violation was the agreement of the tied house. Second was that the house was mismanaged. The Judge did not agree that the house was tied. There seemed to be great difficulty in keeping a public house in a place like this town. He also said that he had some problem pronouncing the name Llanhilleth.

The plaintiff Mr Evans seemed to think that he was entitled to the forfeiture of the lease because he could not get a beefsteak and chips when he called at the Central. The Judge also stated that two gentlemen complained that they could not get accommodation at the pub, and he thought they were fortunate, as there were about 200 miners present on a payday. There were also half a dozen trains passing close by every day. He also said that the Hotel was a drinking place for miners and as the barrellage had gone up and not down, how could the Hotel be mismanaged. The Jury retired for a few minutes and returned a verdict in favour of Mr Simmonds.

The Judge Lawrence in this case was the same Judge Alfred Tristam discussed in an earlier chapter who was born in Pontypool.

During the First World War the brewery had trouble keeping key workers, some volunteered to serve King and Country while others were called up and it was these workers who faced a tribunal in order to remain at the brewery.

J Edgar and his directors still maintained a profit throughout these difficult years. Nett profits were around £11,000 and £14,000. A five year average for pre war years was £14,000.

John Edgar Webb died at Larkfield House on St David's Day, March 1st 1918. He died in his sleep and his wife Margaret Annie found him dead when she brought him his morning cup of tea. The cause of death was cancer.

By the time of J Edgar's death, his only daughter Eleanor had married Mr Clifford Morgan whose family was involved in Llanbradach Colliery. The Colliery employed 2500 men in 1916. Its Head Office was Cardiff Collieries Ltd, 6 Bute Street Crescent, Cardiff. Cardiff Collieries also had premises in the London area, and Clifford was sent to manage the London Offices.

Walton Leigh, Addlestone, Surrey.

Edgar Webb's widow was very fond of her only daughter and made a decision to sell Larkfield House so that she could buy Walton Leigh in Addlestone, Surrey to be near her. She hired a private train to take her and her family, also her staff and all their belongings. When she sold the house in Surrey a few years later, to move back to Penylan House in Cardiff, she made the same arrangements to return.

Margaret Annie died on February 14th 1930 her final journey was back to Chepstow to be buried in the family mausoleum at Bulwark Cemetery.

Chapter 4
William Edgar Kenneth Webb 1893-1954

One must wonder if J Edgar had lived to a ripe old age, would any of his sons have made a career at Aberbeeg Brewery. Kenneth, Leslie and Douglas had taken up military posts in the army and even as late as 1921, four years after his father's death, the next Managing Director, Kenneth was living in Cheshire.

William Edgar Kenneth Webb, the eldest son of Edgar became the next and last of the Webbs to run the brewery. Kenneth was born in Llanhilleth House, Llanhilleth and ,was educated at Clifton Preparatory School. He was interested in sport and played 1st team football and cricket. He went on to Sherbourne School in Dorset where he was house captain in the senior house. The final part of Kenneth Webb's education was at Exeter College, Oxford and again he was very active in the sports, playing hockey and golf for Oxford.

Kenneth Webb served in France from January 1915 with the Royal Army Corps. He was invalided home in February 1917 and discharged from the Army with a leg wound in September of the same year. In 1917 he also joined the staff of Partington Steel and Iron Company in Manchester.

During his time in the forces or perhaps whilst living in Cheshire, Kenneth Webb made friends with Mr Alf Bradshaw. In correspondence from Kenneth Webb to his friend, the reference is always 'Dear Bradshaw' suggesting military superiority, but written with genuine intent. Alf was offered a job at the Aberbeeg Brewery as a mechanic and driver which must have been much appreciated in the gloomy days of 1923. The duties were to include maintaining the company's two Ford trucks and two Sentinel steam wagons. For the period, the wage offered of £4 per week and a daily beer ration of $4\frac{1}{2}$ pints was very acceptable and so Alf Bradshaw's career with the brewery commenced. A bond of friendship between the two, one a company director, the other a respectful employee, lasted throughout their lives.

When Kenneth Webb died in 1954, his widow Anita presented Alf with her husband's watch as a token of the family's respect for his service to the Company.

Upon leaving the brewery after many years service, Alf and his wife Kitty became landlords of the Royal Oak in Cwm and The Globe at Abertillery. Alf passed away during the winter of 1958 and such was the respect that the Webb family had for him, that a number of them made their way from Anglesey to Abertillery to attend the funeral.

On March 2nd 1918, the day after his father John Edgar died, Kenneth was made a director of Webbs Aberbeeg Ltd. The next important stage of his life was on the 18th December 1918 when he married Anita Lloyd of West Kirby, Wirral, Cheshire. The reception was held at the Lloyd's family home Oatland House. Anita Lloyd's father was Colonel John Evans Lloyd. The colonel had commanded the King's Liverpool's in France during World War One, he was also Sheriff of Anglesey from 1935 to 1936. By 1938 he was the chairman of Webbs Aberbeeg Ltd.

Colonel Lloyd's other daughter married Lord Leverhulme. Kenneth Webb was made Managing Director of Webbs in 1922 while he was living at Thornton Hough, Cheshire.

In 1922 Kenneth and Anita Webb moved into the Washington Hotel, Penarth. This enabled them to go house hunting in the Lisvane area near Cardiff and Kenneth and his family moved into Highmead House in about 1925. Jean Rosemary Webb was born on 13th May 1926. Avril Margaret Webb was born in 1922 but died of pneumonia in 1930, an event which devastated the family. The first boy for Kenneth and Anita was John Anthony born in 1928.

Kenneth Webb's other daughter Merle remembers Christmas 1929 when a family reunion took place and they met at Margaret Annie Webb's home, a lovely house with an impressive hall complete with palm trees. The adults numbered 13, an unlucky number so Merle was invited to dine with the adults, much to the envy of the other children who had to dine

Kenneth Webb and his bride Anita Lloyd.

with their nannies. It was also remembered by Merle as her grandmother's last Christmas, Margaret Annie Webb died on 14th February 1930.

The family living next to the Webbs at Lisvane were called Gaskell. The Gaskell family had been involved in the Hancocks Brewery Cardiff since its early days. By the time Kenneth Webb moved to Lisvane, Gerald Gaskell was Managing Director of the Hancocks Brewery Co. Kenneth's daughter Merle recalls her father referring to the Gaskells running the biggest Welsh brewery while Kenneth managed a small one. Kenneth Webb was actually slightly modest in making this statement.

Brondeg House, Aberbeeg was built for John R Webb and it was situated by the old woodman's cottage. On the other side was a house named The Firs. After John R's widow died the houses were occupied by the brewery staff. John Dixon the head brewer was at Brondeg at one time, he came to Webbs around 1920. Some Aberbeeg locals told that he came from a famous family of brewers, John Dixon was also a well known artist. George Wynne, one-time landlord of the Cwm Hotel, Abertillery remembered going to Mr Dixon at Brondeg for art lessons. George also remembered a religious painting by John Dixon that might have been

47

The Bush Hotel, Abertillery once the flagship of the Webbs hotel chain.

donated to St Michaels Church, Abertillery. John Dixon was also associated with the Aberbeeg rugby team and photographs were often taken of the team at Brondeg or in the brewery yard.

Another faithful employee was William F Burgess. He started with John R in 1899 and was employed as a secretary, one of his hobbies being the study of folklore in the area. This hobby would have kept Mr Burgess quite busy, as the valley people at that time were very superstitious. As anyone who has read the work of Rev Edmund Jones the Old Prophet will agree. The Aberbeeg area was full of stories of ghosts, fairies and other strange events. In April 1937 Mr Burgess was appointed Assistant Managing Director.

Mr O B Matthews joined the Brewery in John Edgar Webb's time around 1911. He was at one time Clerk of Works and whilst carrying out some of his duties he fell sixteen feet and broke his leg. Mr Matthews was a keen amateur photographer and in common with William Burgess, collected information on old time valley folklore.

An Abertillery family called Lewis worked for years at Webbs. Mr Danny Lewis was a carpenter his son Stan also worked there. Stan was a painter and along with another young painter Jack Martindale continued to work at Webbs until they reached retirement age.

The author worked alongside Stan and found him to be a very quiet and gentle man. Stan Lewis and his wife went on the brewery bus trip to Glasgow. On his retirement Stan was given a barometer and a clock.

Jack Martindale like his father before him worked at Webbs. He started in 1926 on a sub contract basis. He was hired to paint The Bush Hotel at Abertillery, The Central Hotel, Llanhilleth and The Hanbury Hotel at Aberbeeg. The time given, was for the work to be completed in three months. Jack knew this time was impossible with the little amount of scaffolding that was provided, but it was the start of a long relationship with the brewery.

In the Depression the top rate was 1 shilling and 5 pence an hour (7p). When painting was slack, Jack was expected to do other work. He delivered beer with a horse and cart and also went out with the Webbs steam traction engines. These engines were very slow, they also had carbide lamps and candles as a form of lighting. Jack's father was Transport Manager and his brother Joe also worked in transport.

At the rear Stan Lewis and Jos Saunders. In the front Jack Martindale, Polly Purchase and Len Smith.

By 1943 Jack was General Foreman and was also in charge of Works Contracts. He became Clerk of Works in 1968 although by this time Webbs had been taken over by Northern Breweries. Jack was almost a walking encyclopedia on Webbs pubs, having painted most of them in his time. He was also familiar with the drainage systems as blocked drains were also part of his work.

Jack and his wife Elsie had a painting and decorating shop adjacent to the Conservative Club in Llanhilleth. Jack retired on 27th August 1973 and was presented with a gold wristwatch for long and faithful service.

In 1919 the Webbs Brewery used horses and draywagons until a meeting on 12th June 1919, when the Brewery Manager John Dixon brought forward the question of delivery of goods. He had spent some time on the subject of transport and after careful consideration, he could no longer recommend horses and was in favour of a steam lorry. He produced an estimate for a Sentinel steam lorry, which he was confident fellow directors would agree to purchase after a test run at the brewery. The estimate was £1260 but also contained a clause allowing the price to rise in the event of a rise in materials before the wagon was delivered to the brewery. The directors agreed to purchase the steam lorry, but asked John Dixon to try to tie the Sentinel Steam Co to the original price of £1260. The vehicle was delivered in the Autumn and the final price was £1290.

At the January meeting in 1920, John Dixon informed the Board that the lorry was working satisfactorily, but to cope with the orders an additional vehicle would be required. It was agreed by the Board to purchase another lorry. The estimate John Dixon had this time was £1340 and in September 1920 a second Sentinel steam lorry was delivered to the brewery. These steam vehicles were a slow way of transport, but quite a few other breweries were using them and in the heart of a coal mining area they were cheap to run. They were used along with other lorries up until the 1940s, even when petrol and diesel trucks had all but replaced steam power. A theory put forward as to why these two steam wagons lasted for such a long time was the outbreak of the Second World war and the rationing of petrol.

One of the steam lorry drivers was a Mr Hiscocks whose nickname was Ginger, the other was driven by a Mr T Thomas. An amusing story must be related concerning the steam wagon driven by Ginger Hiscocks. One day as he returned to the brewery, the steam lorry tipped onto its side near the Old Aberbeeg Club. The result was that Ginger suffered burns and scalding and was taken to Aberbeeg Hospital for treatment. Whilst in hospital it was noted that Ginger was slow to respond to the treatment. He was seen by Dr Scanlon who diagnosed some some form of dehydration. It was agreed to phone the brewery and arrange for Mr

Hiscocks to have his daily beer allowance brought to the hospital. After that Ginger made a complete recovery. This could be a true story because it was a tradition for landlords to give the draymen a pint of beer each time they delivered. Other men who drove the old steam lorry at a later date were a Mr Rowlands and Mr Webber.

In 1924 Webbs received an offer of a merger from Phillips Brewery of Newport. The terms of the merger were discussed and rejected by the Webbs Board of Directors.

The Phillips Brewery Ltd Newport which was on Dock Road, was founded in 1874 and registered in 1892. In 1924 at the time of the offer, it had a few pubs in the Abertillery area. The Castle at Abertillery was a Phillips pub, situated on the corner of Castle Street and Hill Street now since demolished. In the 1940s it was run by the Walters family and by Frank and Joan Blackmore in the early fifties. The Bell at Abertillery was another and the Walters moved into the Bell from the Castle. Other Phillips pubs were the Rolling Mill Abertillery, The Bridgend Penybont, the Walpole Llanhilleth and the Coach and Horses at Six Bells.

The Coach and Horses was run by Sid Martin in the 1950s and was situated by the entrance to Arael Griffin Colliery and was kept quite busy by the miners coming off the afternoon shift.

Phillips were taken over in 1949 by Simmonds of Reading and the Newport Brewery ceased brewing in 1968. Simmonds were themselves taken over in 1960 by Courage Breweries.

In 1927 Leslie Webb joined the brewery at Aberbeeg, he was the younger brother of Kenneth. He was born at Hafodafol House in Nantyglo in 1897, his full name being John Leslie Symons Webb. He was educated in the same public school as his brothers Martin, Kenneth and Geoffrey, first at Clifton Prep School and then at Sherbourne School in Dorset.

On leaving school Leslie Webb went directly into Officers Training Camp at Abergele in North Wales. On leaving the Abergele Camp he went on to serve as a Lieutenant in Mesopotania. He was torpedoed twice, the first time when a destroyer came alongside the troopship to transfer troops. The destroyer was hit by a torpedo and many men fell between the two ships and were crushed to death. The second time, all Leslie could remember was being alone on a life raft when he was rescued.

A great friend of Leslie Webb was Walter C Phillips. The Phillips family had a Tent and Marquee Business in Newport. Both men were in Mesopotania but neither man was aware of it, until one night Walter opened up the flap of Leslie's tent and shouted in 'Hello Leslie', and so two gallant friends were suddenly re-united.

The region was a terrible place to serve in with temperatures of 130 degrees Fahrenheit in the shade. The Turks fought with great ferocity and

51

the British suffered appalling losses.

Leslie Webb was returning home on a troopship when he received a telegram informing him of his father's death on 1st March 1918.

Leslie married Emma Muriel Berry on 22nd July 1928 and his brother Martin married Emma's sister Elizabeth. So, just as John Richard and Tom Alexander Webb had married the Davies sisters of Nantyglo, history was repeated with the Webb brothers and the Berry sisters. Leslie and Emma had three children, Michael who was born in 1929, Maureen in 1935 and John Edgar Richard in 1939.

At a board meeting in the summer of 1928 Kenneth Webb read a letter from the Andrew Buchan Brewery board of Directors. 'We the undersigned Directors, have invested the proposals for an amalgamation of Webbs Aberbeeg Ltd, with Andrew Buchan Breweries Ltd, embodying the voluntary liquidation of Webb Aberbeeg Ltd, and the payment by Buchans of Webbs mortgages, Bank debentures holders and shareholders by means of cash or preferred shares in Buchan Breweries.'

This picture shows Manchester House and Lou Poole's shop on the left and the Hanbury on the right.

The Webbs board then concluded -

'After careful consideration we hereby resolve that the proposal cannot be entertained by us, and we are not prepared to submit the proposals to the debenture and the shareholders of the Company.

Having taken into account the drastic reductions proposed to be made in the Capital Debentures and Mortgages of this Company, while at the same time no corresponding reductions in the proposed capital of Buchans.'

'Signed'
John E Lloyd
Fredrick Hawkins
WEK Webb
J Leslie S Webb

The Andrew Buchan Brewery was started by the Rhymney Iron Co, in 1839. As his name implies, Andrew Buchan was a Scotsman. Buchan was the manager of the brewery supplying beer for the ironworks workforce and also pubs in the surrounding area. He retired in 1869 and died the following year at the age of 82. He was buried in Rhymney Churchyard and his funeral was the largest ever seen in the Rhymney area. By 1875 William Pritchard was the manager. He remained manager until 1898 when in a depressed state of mind, he shot himself in the brewery railway sidings. William Pritchard's nephew Francis then became manager but by 1900 he had left the Company having purchased the Western Valley Brewery at Crumlin.

In 1920 the Powell Duffryn Co. acquired the Rhymney Iron Co., the Brewery Manager was Mr G L Pares. It was Mr Pares who was in charge

Andrew Buchans Brewery, Rhymney later renamed Rhymney Brewery.

53

of the Buchan Brewery at the time of the suggested merger with Webbs in 1928.

By March 1929 Buchans were negotiating a deal with Griffiths Brothers Ltd of Blaina. The Griffiths Brewery had about 28 pubs in the surrounding area with six in Blaina. The Brewery was registered in September 1890 and it had twenty licensed houses. It went into liquidation on 18th August 1909 but resumed trading on 7th July 1910.

In June 1930 The Andrew Buchan Brewery took over the D Francis Pritchard Brewery at Crumlin. So once again D Francis Pritchard was in the employment of Andrew Buchans Brewery Rhymney. On one of the Pritchard stone bottles there was a family coat of arms. It consisted of a wheatsheaf, swords and spears and a racehorse. Underneath was the motto Purity and Clarity.

A member of the Pritchard family spent some time in designing a character based on the racehorse, in the form of a beer barrel with a jockey sitting on the barrel with the slogan The True Brew always in good condition. This trademark was used by Buchans at a later date and called the Hobby Horse. So Webbs Aberbeeg Ltd now faced Buchans operating in Blaina and also at Crumlin Brewery, mergers being quite common in the 1920s and 1930s. All the South Wales breweries had suffered continual reductions in sales and by merging with other breweries, hoped to be stronger and better able to fight the opposition.

Crumlin Viaduct with the D F Pritchard Brewery below.

54

At the time of the Buchans offer, Kenneth Webb had been in charge for ten years, and it had been ten of the most difficult years the Webb family and the brewery had faced. Troubled times started after World War One. During the war the government took control of the mines but they were returned to the coal owners when hostilities ceased in 1918.

A royal commission was set up in 1919 to investigate the problems of the coalfield, it was headed by Sir John Sankey. The commission, after taking in all the facts came out on the side of nationalisation of the coalfields, but the Liberal Government under Lloyd George would not agree. As some of the European coalfields recovered from the effects of the war, demand for Welsh coal dwindled. The coal-owners were now receiving less for their coal and the miners were expected to work for less money. Things came to a head during the winter of 1920-21. A triple alliance between miners, railwaymen and transport workers was formed and a strike was called for the 15th April 1921. But this alliance broke down with a climbdown by the railwaymen and transport workers and 15th April became known as Black Friday.

Llanhilleth Colliery which was in operation from 1870 until 1968.

The miners fought on alone with their families suffering great hardships but they finally gave up on 1st June 1921.

In 1926 another commission was set up to consider the future of the coalfields and the miners.

The findings of the Samuel Commission was for a programme of modernisation and a better welfare system. But wage cuts of 25% was the price the miners were asked to pay. The coal-owners then threatened the miners with a lockout if they did not accept the cuts. With the backing of the T U C, the miners resisted and the now famous battle cry, 'not a penny of our pay, not a minute on the day' rang out in the valleys. The General Strike was called for 4th May but by 12th May it had collapsed and once again the miners were fighting alone. The miners fought an heroic battle, with families and whole communities suffering great hardships. Many families left the valleys looking for a better life for their children, but many stayed to fight for another six months before finally giving up the struggle.

So, it was against this background of upheaval that Kenneth Webb and most other Welsh breweries found trade falling.

In 1927 Kenneth Webb informed his fellow directors of a trade reduction of 35% as a result of the 1926 General Strike and also three collieries closing as a result of the strike in the Abertillery area.

Managing a brewery in the 1920s was not an easy task but life for the working man outside the brewery was even worse. Almost every couple of weeks one colliery or another had disputes and strikes. When this happened the management would send the men home and of course

Cwmtillery Colliery

they would receive no pay. There were a lot of geological faults and floodings in the collieries and some pits were susceptible to the floodings more than others. One of these was the pit at Aberbeeg, the property of Budd & Co.

The same year as Kenneth Webb made his speech to his Board of Directors, The Marine Colliery of Cwm, not more than three miles away, on March 1st, experienced an underground explosion claiming the lives of 52 men and boys and leaving many widows to fight to survive and raise their families. Some victims of the disaster were so badly burnt that identification was almost impossible. One boy who survived the explosion was Ted Button, but when he found that his brother was still in the mine, he ventured back into the workings only to become another victim himself. Such was the spirit and bond of the Welsh miners for their brothers and each other.

The early 1930s brought more misery throughout South Wales, although the government did start to create special areas for development. Factories were built at Treforest, Bridgend and Hirwaun. These areas did help to reduce unemployment but only on a small scale.

Major John Martin Webb a grandson of J Edgar Webb related a story about Webbs and canned beer.

During the early 1930s the tinplate industry was in deep recession, a couple of Welsh breweries, in an effort to alleviate the problem spent a lot of money developing canned beer. However, continued research has not provided firm evidence to substantiate the J M Webb story. A couple of breweries in 1934 were known to have been interested in canned beer and a fierce battle between two Llanelli companies namely Buckleys and Felinfoel Brewery are recorded, with Felinfoel Brewery becoming the first in December 1935 to produce canned beer, followed closely by Buckleys. The can Felinfoel produced looked very much like a 'Brasso' tin, some of these cans have survived and are very collectable. The canned beer story was handed down to John M Webb by his father Martin Webb. Although neither John M Webb or his father Martin actually worked at Webbs Aberbeeg, the story is so closely related to the time and effort spent in trying to revive the tinplate industry, it is reasonable to accept the theory. John M Webb also stated that Webbs Aberbeeg Ltd, lost a great deal of money in the canned beer venture. From 1936 to 1937 Webbs and most other breweries began to recover from early 1930s depression and by 1938 was ready to celebrate its centenary year in style. A trip to the Empire Exhibition Glasgow was organised by Webbs for its staff and employees, also included were the wives. An excursion to Barry Island was also arranged as part of the celebrations. Another gesture was the provision of seats outside the Hanbury Hotel for the people of Aberbeeg to sit and rest. The board of Directors at the time of the celebrations consisted of Kenneth Webb, Leslie Webb, Col John E Lloyd, Col J Frederick Hawkins and Mr W E Burgess. By now Webbs beer was a household name in the county and

A line up of Directors and Staff taken in front of Brewery Terrace in 1938, to celebrate 100 years of brewing. Leslie and Kenneth Webb are 4th and 5th from the left in the front row.

the Company also acted as agents for Whitbread bottled beers, Seager & Evans wines & spirits, Nicholson Gin, Vile Bros mineral waters, Bulmers Ciders, Churlton Wines & Spirits, Rigby & Evans Wines & Spirit, Gaskell & Chambers beer engines, Duttsons & Knight sugar, Robson malt, Thornberry hops, Harvey Steel sugar, Adlams beer plant, Baileys malt, Paines sugar, C H Bevan hops and Ipswich Malting Co malt.

In 1939 and with World War Two about to begin, Kenneth Webb confided his worries about the future of the brewery to his daughter Merle. Would he be able to get the hops, malt and other ingredients to brew, also fuel to run the lorries and the possible loss of staff as in World War One?

One man to find employment in the brewery in 1939 was Mr Arthur Kimber. He was born and bred in Aberbeeg, but he was working away from home when war broke out and Arthur decided to give up his job in Birmingham and head home. He started work in Webbs Brewery in October 1939 and went into the bottling stores, his boss was Mr Thomas. Mr Thomas was a keen cross country runner and he also trained Aberbeeg rugby team.

The bottling equipment at this time was very primitive, bottles being placed on trays which were dipped into a tank. The trays were then lifted and the bottles further cleaned by use of a hand brush. The bottles were taken to a twelve-head filler and filled, crown corked one at a time and labelled by hand.

The first girls to start work in the bottling department were Susan Ferris and Violet Norris in April 1940. If one worked for Webbs around this time, and unless specialised in one job, employees were expected to be adaptable, thus Arthur Kimber also spent time in the offices, cellars, washyard and brewing department. The old wooden barrels were washed and steamed and put out in the wash yard and if stubborn bits remained inside the barrels, a chain was put inside and it was bowled around the yard until it was clean.

The day before brewing, the malt was crushed and put on a belt and conveyed up to the grist bins. The following morning at 6am, the brewer would mash it by dropping the crushed malt down into two mash tuns, adding sugar and other ingredients. Sparge pipes would rotate, dripping boiling water onto the crushed malt. The liquid would then flow into the coppers, this was known as the wort. At 2pm on brew days, the mash tuns would be finished. By this time the grains would be steaming hot and had to be cooled before removal. One man then stripped to the waist, would get into the mash tun and shovel the spent grains onto a conveyor belt and into a tank. Local farmers used to buy grain and transport it with their horses and carts and later with tractors. Albert Francombe and his brother George worked in Webbs in the early 1940s. George was a good

On the right is Arthur Kimber surrounded by his bottling staff.

welterweight boxer and he fought some of the best boxers in the country at his weight. George was allowed to train in a room upstairs in the Hanbury Hotel and if he needed to lose weight, he would be the one to empty the grain out of the mash tuns.

In 1941 Arthur Kimber was called up for active service and joined the Air Force. He married Susan Ferris who worked in the bottling and just prior to their marriage, Kenneth Webb gave Arthur a five pound note as a present. By 1942 standards this was a substantial sum. Arthur returned to the brewery in 1947 and went back to the bottling store.

In the early 1950s a new bottling store was built with cold rooms and an automatic bottling plant. Arthur Kimber became bottling foreman and later manager with a staff of 4 men and 16 to 18 women. The new plant could produce 600 bottles per hour, this included washing, examining bottles for foreign bodies, pasteurisation of bottles for longer shelf life and labelling. The beer included Golden and Special Ales, 1/2 pint bottles and Strong Ale in flagons. They were also agents for Tennents Barley Wine and bottled Manns and Guinness under licence. The Guinness came up to the brewery sidings by tram in special vats. It was then pumped into the brewery container to settle before bottling. When beer 'went off' it was returned to the brewery and known as ullage and tipped into a tank, when the tank was full the Customs and Excise officers came and measured the amount for Tax and Duty purposes. The waste beer was then discharged into the river and on these days a white froth was seen floating on the water for hundreds of yards. Webbs had an occasional warning and summons for this practice, which on reflection seems odd when you imagine the coal dust and iron deposits already in the river. The water for the brewery came from Cwmbeeg Dingle, the dingle being a place for locals to picnic and pick whimberries. At one time Janto Wilding had a small cottage situated in Cwmbeeg Dingle and the brewery paid him a sum of money to keep the end of the brewery pipe clear of sludge.

Don Probert left school and went to work for Webbs in 1940, serving as as apprentice with the painters. He then served time in the forces and returned to Webbs when he was demobbed. As well as being a first class painter, he was also a signwriter for Webbs. He remembers one visit to W J Jones' office. W J was a stickler for detail and he did not like some of the Webbs signs, or the way they were written, in W J words they were very disjointed and spidery. Don Probert was given the task of producing something more flowing. A few days later Don produced for W J a new style and it was used continually thereafter.

Don Probert's talents as a signwriter kept him very busy. A lot of pubs, with sound pine ends were used to advertise 'Webbs Clearly the Best' even the north pine end of the brewery was used.

Pictured above are examples of the old and revised logo.

At one time a lot of Webbs pubs had cast iron tables with hardwood tops and the author remembers one job at the Hafodyrynys Hotel. Jack Martindale asked Don Probert to pick out with enamel paints, the features on these tables, usually Britannia with her trident and shield. This was quite a painstaking job considering the pub had between 20 and 30 tables. When Jack Martindale retired in 1973, Don was made Clerk of Works and he held this post until he retired in 1983.

Aberbeeg looking south with Aberbeeg rugby ground and Railway Terrace.

On the left is Don Probert with colleague Fred Legge, pictured at the rear of the Cwm Hotel, Abertillery.

In the front are Don Probert, Ivor Woodruff and Stan Lewis. Standing are John Williams and George Pick. Unfortunately it has not been possible to trace the lady in the centre.

Don was a cheerful man always telling jokes and he had a passion for horse racing. He loaned the author a few photographs for this book and when looking at the back of one of the pictures, it was like looking at a betting slip with the horses names on it!

March 12th 1941 was the day that Colonel John E Lloyd was killed in an air raid. He was living at the time in Brentwood House, Eleanor Road, Bidston near Birkenhead. Two German sea mines missed their intended targets completely and demolished the house. The colonel, his cook, parlourmaid and head gardener had taken refuge in the cellar but they were all killed. One housemaid who had a half day off and did not return until the next day, found the property in ruins. The Colonel's daughter Anita and her husband were devastated by this tragedy.

Col. Lloyd was the Brewery Chairman with vast business experience, and along with Colonel Frederick Hawkins, a brewery director from Reading, both men had guided Kenneth Webb through his days as Managing Director. Col. Fred Hawkins became a Brewery Director by marrying Florence Webb, a daughter of Tom A Webb and Emily Webb nee Davies. At this time Kenneth Webb was still living at Highmead and his brother Leslie lived nearby at a house called Winncoarttes, both brothers were allowed by the board to have a chauffeur. Kenneth used Ted Love and sometimes Gwyn Broome. Kenneth's daughter Merle remembers her sisters always found it amusing when their mother opened the door and greeted Ted with a 'Good morning Love'.

Colonel John E Lloyd in full military uniform. Father-in-law to Kenneth Webb, Colonel Lloyd was a very well respected Webbs Director.

Another duty Ted Love and Alf Bradshaw performed was at holiday time. Both men went to Anglesey by car while the Webb family travelled by rail in a private carriage at the rear of the train. It was disconnected at Chester and re-connected to the Anglesey train. The Webb family stayed at the Red House Rhosneigr, the house that John Edgar Webb had built in 1902. The drivers' duties included not only driving but also rowing, as both the Webb brothers were first class fishermen and both represented Wales in fishing competitions.

Ted Love died many years ago but his family are still involved in the Flyover Garage at Aberbeeg and Crumlin Auto Salvage.

Leslie Webb and his family in the 1930s.

In 1942 the firm Webbs Aberbeeg Ltd went public and in one newspaper of the time came this report.

'Three Sons Who Made Good'
The biggest financial operation connected with the South Wales Brewing Industry for many years is investing more than £3,000,000 in response to a share offer issue by Webbs Aberbeeg Ltd, Aberbeeg Brewers, allotments which were made last week. Behind the firm's success is the story of three sons who made good when their father gave them £1,000 each and some good advice at the

beginning of the last century. One son settled at Birmingham and founded a glassworks, another at Stourbridge to become a seed merchant and the third started a village brewery, now a great industry.

So in 1942 the story of the three sons is going strong, but if we look back, William Webb's father John was a land agent from around 1805 working for Walter Landor Savage at Llantony and he worked at Llantony until his death in April 1848. When the author was first told the story, Aberbeeg locals included also, Webbs machinery eg. lawn mowers so there could have been four sons, also we now know when William Webb married Harriet Walker, he was a rollturner in an ironworks. If John Webb did give his three or four sons a thousand pounds each, at the time, this would represent a huge some by today's standards.

A fine view of old Aberbeeg in about 1910.

Chapter 5

Time to Expand

29th July 1942 - Western Mail

Webbs Aberbeeg Ltd
The Ocean Trust Co Ltd and Associates have purchased the Ordinary Share
Capital of Webbs Brewery Aberbeeg. Major F Beddington Behrens M C
Chairman and Mr Basil M Lindsay Finn R C A Directors of Ocean Trust Co Ltd,
have been invited to join the Webbs Board of Directors.

It was in 1942 that Leslie Webb resigned from the Webbs Board of Directors. At the time of his resignation he and his family were living at Lisvane but shortly after they moved to the Isle of Anglesey and took up residence in the Red House at Rhosneigr, the house built by his grandfather. Leslie was now able to pursue his hobbies to the full especially his favourite which was fishing. He was to die in his sleep on March 13th 1983 aged 85 and is buried with his parents at Chepstow.

From 1942 onwards the day to day decisions were carried out at the offices at Aberbeeg, but the major resolutions were made at 99 Park Lane, London. Kenneth Webb's house at Lisvane was taken over by the Ministry of Food, he then buying a house in north Wales at Llanwrst. The house was situated in the lovely Conway Valley and named Maenen Abbey, but the family never actually moved in due to a number of problems, one of which was the water supply. Maenen Abbey was again put up for sale and after some considerable time it was eventually sold.

Anita Webb moved to Anglesey to help out with the W V S, taking a mobile canteen around various camp sites.

Kenneth Webb moved into The Angel Hotel at Abergavenny travelling to and fro to Aberbeeg and also once a month to Park Lane meetings. In 1944 Webbs took over Ridler & Sons Ltd, cider makers of Hereford & Worcester. The main objective was to sell the cider in the valley pubs because of its relatively cheap price and no tax charge. It was Dick Ridler who owned the Cider Works and over the next few years he became quite friendly with Kenneth Webb. Dick Ridler was also asked to attend the London meetings. During Christmas 1942 the Webb family came to The Angel in Abergavenny for a family reunion. In December 1943 Kenneth and Anita Webb celebrated their Silver Wedding at The Angel. It was in the summer of 1944 that Dick Ridler took the Webbs to view a house near Alfrick in Worcester, the house was Hopton Court. The family liked what they saw, bought it and by October had moved in.

After the Second World War, Webbs Aberbeeg Ltd purchased another company called William Evans & Co (Hereford & Devon) Ltd, Cider and Pectin Manufacturers and in August 1946 they also purchased the David John Pentre Brewery.

Major E Beddington Behrens, Webbs Chairman gave net profits for the Brewery up to 30th September 1945 as £88,710 subject to tax and it was an improvement on the 1944 figure of £78,672.

In 1943 Webbs had its new board of Directors Major F Beddington Behrens, Mr Basil Lindsay Finn, Mr Kenneth Webb and Mr Wm. J Jones. By March 1943 at a meeting at 99 Park Lane London, Major Beddington proposed that Mr Wm. J Jones be elected as Managing Director of Webbs Aberbeeg. The proposal was seconded by Kenneth Webb and by July 1943 Kenneth Webb put forward his intentions to retire as General Manager. It was agreed to accept this but he would still remain as a Director and Technical Advisor. Mr Wm. J Jones remained at Aberbeeg until the early 1960s. Also in 1943 a new brewer came to Aberbeeg a Mr F B Wright and he remained there for many years. He was originally from Stockport.

In early 1944, Webbs were looking for new advertising ideas. Kenneth Webb's daughter Merle told the author that her father was at a meeting to discuss new material when a young man tossed a card on the directors' table with 'Clearly the Best' written on it. The directors all agreed on using it and it was associated with Webbs from that day forward. It is unfortunate that the young man's name is not known but the slogan was a stroke of pure genius. Even today when discussing Webbs, the older generation will still say, oh yes Webbs Clearly the Best. The company used it on beer mats, waiters' trays, ash trays and electric clocks. Also pocket calendars were purchased from Malcolm Campbells Plastics Ltd, 10,000 for a cost of £175.

The following important statement was issued on 15th August 1946.

Webbs Aberbeeg Ltd, Monmouthshire Brewers have decided to issue 20,000 further ordinary shares of 10/- each at 40s per share equal to 20s per ordinary stock unit of 5/- and to offer them to the ordinary stock holders in the proportion of one new 10/- ordinary share for every 28 ordinary stock unit now held. Immediately after each allotment each new 10/- share will be converted into two 5/- units of ordinary stock ranking purpose in all respects with existing stock and entitled to participate in any dividends which may be declared on or after August 13th 1946. Proceeds of this issue and of 40,000 5% Redeemable Cumulative Preference shares of £1.00 each and 50,000 5% Second Redeemable Cumulative shares of £1.00 each which the directors have agreed to issue at 23s 3d per share, are required to purchase of the whole of the issued capital of David John and Co Ltd, brewers and wine and spirit merchants Pentre Rhondda.

So everything was in place to purchase the David John Brewery at Pentre in the Rhondda.

The David John Brewery was in Llewellyn Street. It was registered in September 1888 to acquire the businesses of the Pentre Brewery and John Davies of the Mardy Brewery. It was the only brewery in the Rhondda Fawr Valley and one of the brewery's best known brews was a pint called Pentre Seven. At the time of the Webbs takeover the David John Brewery had about 25 public houses which included the following.

Pentre Hotel Pentre	Alexandre Hotel Pentre
New Inn Pentre	Griffin Inn Pentre
Red Cow Treorchy	Treorchy Hotel Treorchy
Maerdy Hotel Maerdy	Royal Hotel Maerdy
Penfelli Hotel Cwmparc	Boot Inn Dinas
Maxwell Hotel Ferndale	Commercial Hotel Treharris
Hendrewen Hotel Blaencwm	Commercial Hotel Ystrad
Kings Head Ystrad	Greenfield Hotel Ystrad
Baglan Treherbert	New Inn Treherbert
Ifor Hael Inn Llwynypia	De Winton Tonypandy
Great Western Quakers Yard	Four Bells St Athans
Three Horse Shoes St Athans	Hollybush Hotel Hopkinstown
Windsor Hotel Merthyr Vale	

The north side of the Brewery with Brewery Terrace in the background.

One man who had the distinction of working at the two Rhondda breweries and later at Webbs Aberbeeg was Mr Dilwyn Jones of Treorchy. At the end of April 1941 Dilwyn had a Saturday morning job with a local butcher. One Saturday the butcher took young Dilwyn to the David John Pentre Brewery to grind some of his knives. Dilwyn was offered a full time job (one wink of the butcher and with the consent of his parents) and he started the following Monday 3rd May. He became a Junior Clerk and earned 10/- per week (50p). Whilst at David John's his other jobs included helping with deliveries and working in the cellar and bottling stores. Following the 1946 takeover by Webbs, he came to Aberbeeg for a short while but returned to David John's after a few months.

During his time at John's he remembered some of the staff. These included Chairman M D Thomas John, Director and Brewer I L Evans, Chief Clerk W Hughes, Office Manager I Morris, Bottling Stores Manager I Nottingham and Cooper D Phillips.

The main beers were Pentre Seven discontinued in 1941 a Light Ale, Johns Golden Bitter XXXX a dark beer and Excel Stout.

Dilwyn Jones became a salesman for the David John Brewery and when he left the Pentre for Fernvale he took up the position of salesman.

On leaving Fernvale he joined Webbs Aberbeeg, firstly as a salesman and later became Sales Manager. He worked under W J Jones and he was sure that W J came to Webbs from the Buchans Brewery at Rhymney, later to become Rhymney Brewery Ltd. This could well be true as this information was also given to the author by Mrs Dorothy Arndell. Dilwyn also worked at Webbs during the time Mr Sidney Snazell was Managing Director after W J Jones. It was 1983 when Dilwyn Jones retired due to ill health, the Managing Director at that time being Mr Aubrey Jones.

Webbs Brewery Deal - Western Mail August 27th 1949

It is announced by Webbs Aberbeeg Limited that their offer to purchase the shares of Fernvale Brewery Co, has now been unconditional as a result of its acceptance in respect of more than 90 per cent of the issued share capital. The Fernvale Brewery Company has an issued share capital of £33,983 in ordinary shares of £1 each and carries on business at Pontygwaith, Rhondda.

Rise
Webbs Aberbeeg Ord 18/1/2 up 4d
Fernvale Ord   13/41/2 d up 1/2d

70

At the time of the takeover the Fernvale Brewery had a number of pubs, these included.

Bush Clydach Vale   Rhondda Ferndale
Wheatsheaf Llantrisant   Wyndham Arms Treherbert
The New Inn Llantwit Fardre

The only other takeover by Webbs was of the Thomas Ballinger Mineral Water Co Ltd at Monmouth.

Brewing ceased at the David John Pentre Brewery and the brewery was closed in November 1952, some of the older employees taking early retirement and some others were transferred to the Fernvale Brewery. As 2nd June 1953 approached the whole nation made preparations to celebrate the young Queen's Coronation. Street parties were organised and towns and villages were decked out with flags and bunting. Webbs Aberbeeg also made plans to celebrate. Flags were put up in most pubs, a Coronation Ale was discussed at one of the Directors meetings but it was decided not to brew the beer at Aberbeeg, but give the order to the Ind Coope Co Ltd. The Coronation Ale came in small half pint bottles.

The Directors of Webbs also placed an order with Cornfield Ltd of London for 1,000 water jugs with Webbs Clearly the Best inscribed and 1,000 with Fernvale Ales, the Pride of Wales. The jugs were made by Wade & Co and both jugs showed a young picture motif under the spout and cost 3s 6d each (17½ p).

During 1953 and into 1954 Kenneth Webb's health deteriorated and he missed quite a few board meetings. At one meeting fellow directors allowed him an absence of leave with pay.

Kenneth and Anita Webb.

Kenneth Webb's daughter Merle stated that at one time her father smoked between 60 and 70 cigarettes a day, most photographs in fact show him with a cigarette.

William Edgar Kenneth Webb died on 1st November 1954 at the University Hospital in London. Cause of death was respiratory failure and chronic intestinal pulmonary fibrosis. He was 61 years old.

Kenneth Webb's other achievements in life besides managing the brewery included:

A Member of the Brewers Council London
A Member of the General Committee National Trade Welfare
　　Association London
A Member of the Finance Committee National Trade Defence
　　Association London
A Member of the Executive Committee National Trade Defence
　　Association London
Vice Chairman of the Monmouthshire Brewers Association
Vice Chairman of the South Wales National Trade Defence Association
Local Director of the Law and Union Rock Ins Co
Member of the Racecourse Committee Chepstow
Vice President of the Llandaff and Barry Conservative Association
Deputy Chairman of the Llanishen and Lisvane Conservative
　　Association

Kenneth Webb was the last member of the Webb Family to be involved in the Aberbeeg Brewery.

So ended a tradition which had lasted for 116 years.

Six Bells Colliery, Abertillery

On July 6th 1960 the directors of Webbs Aberbeeg Ltd following a meeting at Cardiff decided to donate £500 to the Six Bells Disaster Fund. The fund was set up for the dependants of the 45 miners who died in the Six Bells Colliery explosion on Monday June 28th 1960.

The Six Bells Colliery was sunk in 1891 by John Lancaster & Co and known as Arael Griffin Colliery.

The explosion occurred in the 'W' district situated about 1$1/4$ miles from pit bottom. A national appeal was launched and over £1,000,000 was raised. In 1995 near the colliery site, a fitting memorial to the 45 brave miners who tragically lost their lives was erected.

At the same meeting Mr B M Lindsay Finn reported that following an approach by Northern Breweries of Great Britain and subsequent divisions between himself and Northern Brewery representatives, general agreement had been reached on the terms of an offer to the company shareholders which he (the chairman) could recommend to the directors and shareholders for acceptance.

A letter dated 4th July 1960 by Northern Breweries of Great Britain to the directors containing terms to acquire the Issued Share Capital, was produced to the meeting and the offer unanimously accepted by each director.

The Northern Breweries of Great Britain emerged from the Hope & Anchor Brewery Sheffield founded in 1892 and merged with Henry Tomlinson Ltd in 1942. In 1959 a company called Northern Breweries was formed between Hammond United Breweries Ltd, Hope & Anchor Breweries and John Jeffreys & Co Ltd. The name at the time of the Webbs offer had been changed to Northern Breweries of Great Britain Ltd. Mr John Martin Webb recalls that the man behind Northern Breweries was the Canadian, Edward Taylor the owner of Carling Black Label. He formed Northern Breweries to market his lager in Britain. At the same July meeting it was agreed to sell the William Evans & Co Hereford & Devon Ltd, the cider company, to H P Bulmer. A week later at the Angel Hotel Cardiff present were Mr B M Lindsay, Mr Wm. J Jones, Brig H N Leverson Gower, Mr John Hall, Mr A S Johns and Major S A Snazell.

The meeting discussed the breweries' combined results 8 months to May 31st indicating a profit of £209,808. It was also confirmed to sell the William Evans Cider Company to H P Bulmer, for £250,000. The following year Northern Breweries changed its name to United Breweries.

In October 1961 Mr W J Jones gave up his position as Managing Director and became Deputy Chairman. Mr Jones came to Webbs along with the Ocean Trust Company Ltd, when Kenneth Webb made Webbs Aberbeeg Ltd, a public company. He held the position of Managing Director for 18 years and under W J Jones the company, with its programme of expansion, namely the additions of the Rhondda Breweries and the two Cider Works. The 18 years were good years for Webbs Aberbeeg.

W J as he was known to Webbs staff spent a lot of time and energy on increasing the sale of Webbs beer, one scheme was low interest loans to Workingmens Clubs throughout the valleys. Many clubs used the facility to refurbish or expand the size of their premises. But the conditions for these loans were that clubs were tied to Webbs beer and Webbs only.

In 1962 United Breweries merged with Charrington & Co Ltd, through a holding company called Charrington United Breweries. It was about this time that Major Sidney A Snazell became Managing Director of Webbs, he at one time working for a brewery in Shoreditch, the Wentlock Brewery Co Ltd, Wentlock Road.

The Wentlock Brewery was formed in 1893 to acquire Clover Bell & Company. It was taken over by Bass Ratcliffe & Gretton in 1961 and brewing ceased in 1962.

By the time of the memorial service at Lisvane for Kenneth Webb in 1954, Major Snazell was a director of Fernvale Brewery. By 1960 and with the takeover of Webbs by Northern Breweries of Great Britain, he was a Webbs Director. The 1960s was a period of takeovers and mergers, those affecting South Wales included Courage Barclay's takeover of Simmonds of Reading, it was Simmonds who had taken over Phillips of Newport in 1949. Whitbread took control of Rhymney Breweries Ltd in 1966, Mitchell & Butler merged with Bass Ratcliffe & Cretton Ltd in 1961 to form Bass Limited. Charrington and Bass merged in 1967 to form Bass Charrington. In 1968 Bass took over Hancocks of Cardiff together with their 505 tied houses and all other interests.

With Hancocks pubs and the Webbs Fernvale and the David John Pentre pubs totalling around 730, the combination formed a new company, Welsh Brewers and Joseph Gaskell became its Chairman.

As with most new companies, Welsh Brewers soon found problems with over-capacity The Hancocks Brewery at Swansea was one of the first casualties and closed in 1969.

Webbs at Aberbeeg closed in 1969 for brewing, the Fernvale Brewery following in 1970.

A fleet of Webbs delivery trucks stand in the Brewery yard.

Aberbeeg rugby team outside Brondeg House. Two Webbs representatives on this photograph are Mr Mathews on the far left and and far right seated is Mr John Dixon.

The rugby team, winners of the Cyrus Cup in 1938-39. The team is led by Albert Francombe and the picture was taken in the Brewery grounds.

Chapter 6

End of an Era at Aberbeeg

In 1969 bad news reached Aberbeeg, Webbs were to stop brewing. By the following year many of the Webbs logos had been replaced by those of Welsh Brewers. Dray lorries and other vehicles were repainted in Charrington red and chocolate brown. Mr Desmond Smith had the distinction of being the last brewer at Aberbeeg, he having previously worked for the Ind Coope Brewery at Burton-on-Trent. He had also worked at the Budden and Biggs Brewery at Strood in Kent, a brewery Ind Coope had taken over in 1931. Des also spent some time at the Wrexham Beer and Lager Co Ltd which was also an Ind Coope Brewery, absorbed by them in 1949. Whilst working in the Ind Coope Brewery at Burton-on-Trent Des Smith met Mr Harry Pearce, who was a brewer from Fernvale Brewery in the Rhondda and they became friends.

In 1964 Harry Pearce informed Des Smith that Webbs, now in the Charrington Group were looking for a second brewer. Mr Wright, the head brewer was about to retire and Mr Walker would take his place. So Des Smith moved to Aberbeeg in January 1965 and became head brewer when Mr Walker finished. A final word on Mr Wright was that he had been a Webbs Brewer for 22 years and had been credited with formulating

A young Vic Pettet on the left with his father Albert who was Webbs last cooper.

Webbs Golden Ale and Special Ale. These were two of Webbs most popular bottled ales.

Mr Albert Pettet was the last cooper in the Brewery. He had worked at Webbs for around 25 years and was from the London area, his son Victor also worked with him. Towards the 1960s aluminium casks were introduced, so Mr Pettet's job became less demanding, although he kept the old Webbs oak barrels in good repair when they were damaged. When Albert Pettet retired the last barrel he made and his cooper's tools were donated to the Welsh Folk Museum at St Fagans. The Aberbeeg Brewery continued as a distribution centre until 1988, and despite the fact that it no longer brewed or bottled, it was still a complete unit, with its own Managing Director and all complementary staff.

The maintenance department closed in 1983 with senior painters Stan Lewis and Walter Wells, Allen Frampton the plumber, Dennis Williams, bricklayer and plasterer and former painter Don Probert (now Clerk of Works) all being made redundant.

Therefore after 132 years Webbs had now disappeared and Aberbeeg as a village was also in decline. A lot of the older shops had closed, much of the commercial downturn starting in the early 1960s. The railway line up the Eastern and Western Valleys had closed for passenger trains in May 1962 and in the mid 1960s River Row was demolished. In the late 1960s along with the brewery closing a new road was proposed and

A general view of Aberbeeg showing The Square and the railway lines heading for Cwm.

A view of Aberbeeg before the planners had their way. Some familiar landmarks are River Row, Kibby's Stores, Station House, The Stables, The Hanbury House, Manchester House and the Brewery.

involved straightening the road into Aberbeeg. Buildings in its path included the Ivorites Inn a Rhymney Pub, a cottage belonging to Mr & Mrs Tom Beeson, the woodman's cottage (which was one of the oldest cottages in Aberbeeg), Brondeg House, The Firs, the old stables and the blacksmith's shop. These were all demolished to make way for the new road.

The Square looking at the stables and Jim Bolt's blacksmith shop.

As the years went on the decline of Aberbeeg as a thriving busy village gathered pace. The little knot of shops and two houses opposite the Hanbury Arms were taken down to widen the road. This included Kibby's shop formerly Courtney Edmunds, Uncle Lou Pooles Newsagents and Mr Jones the Barbers. Mr Jones had been in Aberbeeg since the 1930s. This left only Manchester House, originally the business premises of Ebenezer Edmunds and family, then at one time a billiard hall and lastly used by Kibbys as a shop, before eventual conversion into flats. Kibbys original shop was situated next to River Row and had been demolished. Cooks shop, the other side of the river is still standing today and is now used as a hairdressers and post office.

The Aberbeeg Old School and School house were also razed to the ground. Lionel Thomas' shop known as the Aberbeeg Emporium and Bakehouse, a couple of houses and a shop at the beginning of Commercial Road were removed to widen the top road. This left the residents of Aberbeeg with a very uninteresting concrete wall.

A few houses in Railway Terrace were taken down because of subsidence from workings of the National Coal Board. Five houses on Pantddu road suffered the same fate.

Worst of all was the new road built in the 1980s from the traffic lights in Crumlin heading north and into Aberbeeg. In its path were Central Road Llanhilleth and Aberbeeg football field, Aberbeeg Social Club and houses.

Two photographs during the demolition of 1990 which was to change the face of Aberbeeg forever.

A new Social Club and Old Age Pensioners Hall were built, but then a monstrosity of a flyover was erected cutting the village of Aberbeeg completely in half. This flyover passed over the top of the garage and railway to meet the road to Ebbw Vale and Abertillery.

Around 1989 Welsh Brewers or Bass Wales & West as they were then known, made ready to move to their new premises. These new premises were above the Garden Festival Site at Ebbw Vale. The Hanbury Inn closed and in the autumn of 1990 the demolition contractors moved in. Bridgend Demolition and Cossletts were the companies to carry out the work. The author recalls one Sunday morning sadly watching the crane with the ball and chain on, along with the JCBs tearing down the external and internal walls of the Hanbury Arms Hotel, the brewery was also levelled. One hundred and fifty-two years of history had gone and there was nothing to mark its passing.

'Aberbeegians' tend to be very passionate when discussing Aberbeeg. Trevor Wilde, and his 'Memorial to Aberbeeg' comes to mind and also Mary Austin's lovely article printed in the Sunday Mirror a few years ago:

The Village of Smells.

'It is still a beautiful village in spite of the many changes. As a child I remembered how each season engendered an excitement of its own. At Spring we looked for tadpoles in the stream near the Ivorites pub. We did not think 'is it safe' as we went up the lovely dingle to fish. We picked catkins and pussy-willow to take to school. The stream ran for miles down between the two mountains. We used to dam it and make ponds deep enough to swim in. We would walk up and watch the sheep being dipped. People would catch the bus to Aberbeeg and bring their picnics to the dingle. May was bluebell time. My mother's favourite present was and still is, an armful of bluebells. The mountain was transformed into a fluffy blue blanket. Bluebells floated for miles and miles and people came from all around to pick them.

Then came the Whitsun Walks. Walking out with the Methodists and meeting the Church on the Square at Aberbeeg. Every child had new clothes to march out. This was followed by tea at the Chapel and games on the village field.

Aberbeeg was a village of smells. The smell of spring of the bluebells and the smell at Christmas when we carried cakes to be baked in the grocer's bakehouse. The smell of Webbs Brewery where local beer was brewed, had a charm of its own.
No more the smell of hops and beer,
No more the Hanbury standing there.
Trees where bluebells used to grow,
Car Park where huts were once in a row.
Yet the charm is not lost by the road so new,
For still the people welcome you.
A little yellow house which once was home,
Still tugs at my being wherever I roam.

Two interior photographs showing some of the Brewery plant which will be a familiar sight to any former Webbs employees who may be reading this book.

A tanker of beer outside The Hanbury. The beer was pumped direct from the tanks into barrels at each pub.

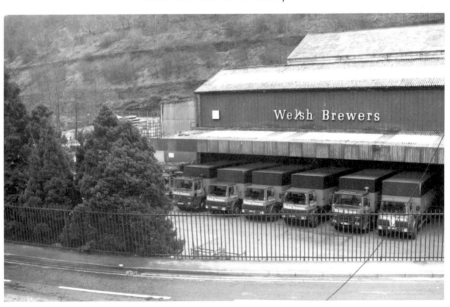

Welsh Brewers drays lined up at the west side of the Brewery.

84

Barrels galore at the north side of the Brewery.

Looking at Aberbeeg from Pantddu Road showing the new Aberbeeg Social Club.

The occasion is Frank Morgan's retirement and those present are Robert Lewis, Mel Jones, Ernie Shepherd, Ron Lawrence, Pat Carter, Albert Rudge, Mrs I Pettet, Mel Burnett, Vic Pettet, Tony Pearce, Desmond Smith (Brewer), Alan Deacon, Dorothy Arndel, Mrs Edwards, Ken Poole, Frank Morgan, Jack Martindale, Joss Saunders, Stan Taylor, E Probert, Ivor Tingle and Albert Pettet.

The Hanbury Hotel, a once familiar landmark in Aberbeeg

Mr Mike Stowermark on duty at Aberbeeg.

*Another chance for a photograph outside the Brewery and on the right is Mr
Len Head and on the left Mr Alan Ruck.*

Chapter 7

Webbs Pubs & People

A function in progress at The Bush Hotel, Abertillery with Directors and Staff of Webbs present.

Webbs sponsored hill climb for Abertillery Wheelers, pictured are John Richards and Les Morgan.

Some more employees and pictured left to right are Jack Martindale, Trevor Vaughan, Charlie Rudge, Roger Rogers, Stan Lewis and Ken Poole.

Jack Martindale outside the Hanbury in Griffithstown.

Alf Bradshaw and his son at a Webbs family function at Malvern.

The Colliers Arms in High Street Abertillery. The pub has now been demolished and has been replaced by the Lloyds Superdrug store. Some former landlords were C Ashley and Polly Purchase.

The Lamb Inn, Abertillery better recognised these days as a carpet shop. Regulars may remember Curly and Dolly Kendall as landlords during the 1950s and 60s.

Two photographs that were taken whilst on a visit to the Guinness works. The group above are pictured in 1961 and the one below is from 1965.

At the corner of Somerset Street Abertillery is The Somerset Hotel. Earlier landlords to be recalled are Mr Samuels and Mr and Mrs Herbert Martin.

An old photograph of the Commercial Hotel in Market Street Abertillery. A one-time landlord was George Winn.

A Brewery night out and some of the lads at the front are Dennis Badham, Harold Challenger, Cyril Jones and Arthur Howells and at the rear are Roy Lewis, Robert Watkins, Graham Pullinge and Ray Brown.

This picture was taken in 1931 at Blackwood Showfield.

Again the venue is The Central at Llanhilleth for a feast in the 1960s.

Most of the lads on this photograph have been named and reading left to right they include A Harries, Wilf Woodland, E Galton, H Rogers, Mr Morgan, Mr Lewis, Mr Lane, Mr G Weaver, Mr Summers, J Hodder, N Hodder, A Strickland and Lou 'The Post' Chivers.

Central Hotel, Llanhilleth. The ladies sat at the front are Mrs English, Mrs Clark. Seated are Mr Protheroe and Bill and Marie Preston. Also included in the photograph are Mrs Creed, Mrs Thomas, Mrs Protheroe, Mrs Holyfield, Mrs Bryant, Mrs A G Thayer, Mr Pople, Mrs Trim, Mrs Thayer, Mrs Jones, Mrs Summers, Mrs Hook and Mrs Catlin.

Another public house in Abertillery no longer with us is the Kings Head. The building however is still in use as commercial premises.

The Railway Inn so named after its close proximity to the one-time railway lines and station in Abertillery. Still a popular public house in the town it is situated opposite Warwills Tin plate Works. This particular photograph shows the premises in the 1950s.

The Castle Abertillery and here we see the landlady Mrs Walters with her successful skittles team.

The Castle skittle team pictured with Mrs Walters and Councillor Derrick.

Llanhilleth Hotel and a landlord who is remembered from many years ago is J B Yewdoll, a long time friend of J R Webb.

The Cwm Hotel which once stood in Alexander Road Abertillery. When the Hotel closed it was initially used for local council offices but these days the site will be better recognised as a block of flats.

Gathered around the table here are, Alan Carter, Pat Carter, Jack and Elsie Martindale, Gwen Lewis, Mrs Brynley Evans, Stan Lewis (standing) and Bryn Evans.

The Tilers Arms Blaina. Although closed for business during recent times the building still stands although a little derelict on the Abertillery Road.

The Six Bells Hotel at Browns Corner showing the distinctive advertisement for Webbs beers.

Webbs extend Christmas Greetings to their Patrons, and hope this coming year will be *Clearly the Best!* **WELSH ALES**

The former Station Hotel Abertillery which has now changed its appearance completely to become the town's rugby club.

Some sporting teams and their trophies at the Clynmawr Hotel. At the rear are Bill Hughes, Frank.Jones, Maureen Hughes, Barney Beatie, Gerald Carpenter and Dave Cecil. Middle row are Bert Pollard, Ron Coles, David Abraham, Jack Cooke and Frank Cecil. Seated in the front are Edgar Bevan and Merv Wicket.

Pictured at the rear are Tom Adams, Ron Dobbins, Len Luker, Alfie York, Brian Paul, Frank Jones, Brian Venn and Bill Hughes. Seated are Ron Donaldson, Bill Hadley and Bill Blacker.

The Red Lion Hotel in the centre of Blaina which is one of the largest licensed premises still in the town.

The White Lion which is still situated in Queen Street Blaina. The landlord at the time of publication is Mr Barrie Davies.

Pictured on a night out are, left to right Brenda Jones, Iris Challenger, Harold Challenger, Cyril Jones, Graham Pullinge, Don Woodward and Sue Woodland.

Some of these faces can be named and they are Bill Taylor, Eileen Taylor, Sue Kimber, Harry Warfield, Mrs Warfield, Mel Burnette and Jean Burnette.

The Clynmawr Hotel standing on Ty Bryn Hill Abertillery. Having had numerous landlords over the years, here are but a few names to recall. Mr and Mrs Gittings during the 1940s, Mr and Mrs Ben Brown and George Jones during the 1950s and Mr and Mrs Bill Hughes from 1963 to 1989.

Standing are Steven Hughes and his father Bill Hughes the landlord. At the front are Martin Price and Barry Dean.

In the centre holding the Toby Taverners Cup for darts is Glyn Howells, being cheered on by Des Smith.

Pictured at the Clynmawr Hotel left to right are Bert Rawlings, Norman Baldwin, Brian Tidy, Ike Millard and Colin Hayes.

Behind the bar and beneath a Webbs clock at the Top Hat Club Cwmtillery are Mr and Mrs Bill Hughes.

Inside another Abertillery hostelry, The Royal Oak and at your service is Mrs Maud Smith.

Two photographs taken inside The Bell at Abertillery. Seen above, behind the bar are Mrs Walters and Mrs Godden and below a few of the regulars.

A popular local boxer from the past was Len Berrow born at Brooklyn Terrace Llanhilleth in 1909. Len fought at lightweight in local boxing booths for Joe Gess and Jack Scarrott.

Long serving landlord and lady at The Central Hotel Llanhilleth Mr and Mrs Creed.

Always a most popular venue for a celebration dinner, The Central Hotel at Llanhilleth and here are two photographs to illustrate some events held there. Readers are invited to start putting some names to the faces.

Some of the Brewery office and administration staff pictured at the plant in 1954.

About to commence dinner are rear, left to right, F Parker, D Johns, Mr Lane, Bill Duggan. Seated R Rice, Mr & Mrs Creed and Mr A Strickland.

Time for a five-minute break for beer and sandwiches and the chosen liquid is Allbright. Pictured are Graham Pullinge and Ray Brown.

The Central Hotel Llanhilleth. On this occasion a presentation is in progress with members of the Monmouthshire Constabulary - Abertillery Division.

The venue is the old Lymes Club Abertillery and the occasion is Joss Saunders' retirement.

Enjoying a night out and a pint are Glyn Howells, Cyril Jones, Len Head, John Courtney, Ron Lawrence, Barry Dean, Ray Jenkins, Gerald Gibbs, Gerald Carpenter, Ray Brown and Trevor Vaughan.

Cup presentations at The Central Hotel Llanhilleth. Left to right are Mr C Williams, Mr T Morgan, unknown, Mr O Rogers, Mr J Hodder, Mr L Denness and Mrs Creed.

The Central Hotel Llanhilleth with another presentation in progress.

The Globe Hotel which was in High Street Abertillery is seen here some forty years ago and since demolished.

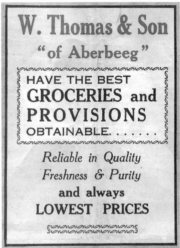

The South Wales Inn is yet another public house no longer standing. This inn was near the old Cwmtillery Colliery.

114

Believed to be a Christmas Party during the 1960s Managing Director Major Sidney Snazell is seated in the centre surrounded by the Brewery staff.

The former Golden Lion in Castle Street Abertillery with the Castle Inn in the background. Len and Maud Smith were your hosts when this picture was taken in the 1950s. Today it goes by the more glamorous name of The Dagmar.

Now demolished, this is how the Royal Exchange will be remembered in Abertillery, once situated opposite Blaenau Gwent Church. Previous landlords and landladies of the Royal Exchange included Mr and Mrs Prosser and Mr and Mrs Ron Lloyd.

Standing are Glyn Davies, Gerald Gibbs, Chris Lowman, Cyril Downes, Pedro Nadal, Tony Padfield, Chris Cordell, Neil Buffin, Elvert Morrisey, Don Woodward, Mel Jones and Alan Morden. Seated are Harry Padfield, Glyn Howells, Len Head and Trevor Padfield.

The Royal Oak Abertillery which was opposite the Globe Hotel and near the Bush. The pub closed in recent years and at the time of publication is up for sale. During the last fifteen years it has been used as a restaurant and Blaenau Gwent Rugby Club. Locals may remember Mr Gwyn Adams and Maud Smith as previous landlords.

The Prince of Wales Hotel was at one time on the hill in the centre of High Street Abertillery. Just one of the many pubs which have closed in the town in recent years, the frontage of the building is hardly recognisable these days and is now converted into a retail shop.

Haydn Morgan and the late Alun Pask enjoy a 'push a penny' game in the Mitre Inn Abertillery.

Another photograph of some customers in the Mitre Inn with rugby personality Haydn Morgan on the right.

An early photograph from the late 1920s or early 1930s of a presentation being made at the Mitre Inn.

This is an advert for the former Webbs Brewery at Aberbeeg in the 1930s

The Webbs Legacy continues today, at the Welsh Brewers Brewery in Cardiff, where quality, history and tradition still foremost in producing the most popular ales in Wales

At the Mitre Inn Abertillery is the darts team with Bobby Parsons holding the cup also in the picture are Des Aylesbury the landlord and Dai Sterry.

Mitre Inn Abertillery. Faces on the photograph include Tom Aylesbury, Dai Davies, Ben Parsons, Albert Poore, Mr Howells and Mel Brewer.

The lady standing is the landlady of the Mitre Inn Dolly Williams, Curly Kendall is far right who was the landlord of the Lamb.

Aptly named The Mitre Inn, this pub is situated on the corner of Mitre Street in Abertillery.

Left to right Brenda Jones, Ann Courtney, Jane Blackmore, Ann Pullinge and Christine Gibbs.

Time for a break. At the back are Doris Larkin, unknown, Mel Burnette and Terry Smith. Seated are Marlene Horler, Eileen Taylor, Olwyn Wilkins, Bett Maggs and Cyril Downes.

The Bottling Girls of the Brewery. Back row Doris Larkin, Bett Pettet, June Leone, Eireen Holyfield, Florrie Larcombe and Thelma ?. Front are Yvonne Fletcher, Marlene Horler, Olwen Wilkins, Glenys James, Sue Kimber and Vi Woodward.

Pictured behind the bar are Arthur Kimber, Nell Daniels, Bett Pettet, Florrie Larcombe and Glyn Rowe.

Chapter 8

Webbs influence around the Valleys

The Royal Oak which is in Station Terrace Cwm. This pub is still open, and one-time landlord was Alf Bradshaw.

Castle Hotel Cwm also on Station Terrace. The back of the pub was almost on the railway line. This pub has since been demolished.

*The Victoria Arms situated in the centre of Cwm, Ebbw Vale. Now a free
house, this was one of the earliest Webbs licensed premises.*

*On the outskirts of Ebbw Vale and pictured here some years ago is the Park
Hotel at Waunllwyd. The appearance of this hotel has changed considerably
since this 40-year old photograph with much work having been carried out in
renovation. This hotel overlooks the Garden Festival site, land itself now being
completely re-developed.*

126

Victoria Hotel Ebbw Vale which was known as the Gin Shop. These premises are now closed.

The Hafodyrynys Hotel as it looked in years gone by with some petrol pumps close by. As with many of the photographs seen in this book, the pubs are still there but the older pictures make interesting comparisons with today's appearances. The Hafodyrynys is now owned by Ushers Brewery Ltd.

The original New Inn at the bottom of Mining School Hill Crumlin. Severe problems with land subsidence resulted in enforced demolition of the pub in the late 1950s and a completely new building was erected. The new 'New Inn' was eventually re-opened in 1961. Also just visible on this photograph is the old Coop Stores, long since gone.

The Newbridge Hotel which stands in the centre of the town still retains its original external appearance if compared with this photograph from the 1950s.

The Plough and Harrow at Pengam.

For those who like
a Bottled Beer

Webbs
GOLDEN
ALE
that's **ALWAYS** CLEAR

*The Tredegar Arms at New
Tredegar.*

The Castle Inn Pontywain. Situated between Cwmcarn and Crosskeys this is now an Ushers Pub.

The Black Lion Hotel Brynmawr which is situated on the Square and now renamed the Talisman.

The Griffin Hotel which once stood in Ivor Street Blaenavon. A Webbs house for very many years, the pub closed in the 1960s the last landlord being Mr Idris Price who held the license for 27 years. The site is now completely re-developed

At one time the town of Blaenavon hosted dozens of public houses and became known as 'the town of pubs and chapels'. Seen above is the Queen Victoria in Prince Street which still survives to this day, having of course been modernised somewhat since this photograph was taken.

The Swan Hotel in Crane Street Pontypool. As with most valley towns Pontypool was not short of licensed premises and the one side of Crane Street alone, housed four inns within a few yards of each other. They were The Swan, The Three Cranes, The Sir Garnet Wolseley and The Ship. All have since been demolished during the last 25 years.

The Webbs house of The Rising Sun still welcomes you on the outskirts of Pontypool at New Inn.

Also on the outskirts of Pontypool at Griffithstown is the three-storey Hanbury Hotel. Pictured here in the 1950s the premises operate under the auspices of Welsh Brewers Ltd.

The Golynos Hotel at Talywain. Demolished in 1960s it stood not far from The Globe.

Another long forgotten public house is The Golden Lion in the main street of Abergavenny. The building is now converted into retail premises.

An old view of the popular Lamb and Flag which is situated on the main Abergavenny to Crickhowell road near the Nevill Hall Hospital.

The Beaufort Arms at Newbridge like several other public houses mentioned in this book has also changed its name since this picture was taken. It is now more readily known as The Trecelyn.

The Tredegar Arms which is still open and situated on Morgan Street near the Tredegar Clock.

The Blacksmiths Arms Inn Mynyddislwyn. Closed in 1994 it is now a private dwelling.

The White Hart Inn at Pentwynmawr near Pontllanfraith which will not be easily recognisable by today's readers. This is the old building which was virtually demolished and replaced by the modern designed pub which stands on the site now.

Chapter 9

More Pictures of Aberbeeg & District

As part of the centenary celebrations of Webbs Brewery, the company organised an excursion for the employees' children to Barry Island. This picture shows the crowds gathered at the brewery entrance on August 9th 1938 before departure.

Christchurch Aberbeeg photographed shortly after its opening in 1910. Inevitably a number of gravestones have been placed in the grounds since this early view and some new houses have been built close by.

A typical valley view with terraced houses stacked on the steep mountainside.

Pen-y-Graig Terrace and Aberbeeg Road.

A view from the hilltops which has changed significantly. Included here are Ty Graig School, Brynithel, some former terraced housing and the once busy railway sheds of Aberbeeg. Also to be seen on the right is Glandwr Farm.

Pantddu Farm looking south, in the background are the bungalows and Llanerch Terrace. Pantddu was farmed in the 1940s by Ben Thomas, then Mr and Mrs Ernie Shephard and at the present day by Clive Gardiner.

Aberbeeg Hospital which overlooks the valley was first opened for patient care in September 1922. There being no such institution as a National Health Service in those days, the hospital was funded by generous voluntary contributions mainly from local colliery employees. Today it specialises in the care of the elderly.

A group of workmen at Christchurch Pendarren Road. The picture has been supplied by the Rudge family of Brynithel, with grandad Rudge in the centre row, fourth from the left.

A photograph from Llanhilleth showing three streets. Hafodarthen Road on the left, Blaencuffin Road on the right and Troy Terrace on the far left.

The Woodman's Cottage near Cwmbeeg Dingle, one of the oldest cottages in Aberbeeg. It was last occupied by Ike Waters and his family, the cottage later to be demolished to make way for the new road.

The New Zealand All Blacks' visit to Webbs Brewery in 1953. Included in the picture are Mr W J Jones the Managing Director and Mr Wright the head brewer.

Members of Aberbeeg Football Club pose for a photograph with their shield at the Hanbury Hotel. Included in the photograph are Vic Pettet, Albert Williams, Mel Smith, Graham Pullinge and Terry Tucker.

Aberbeeg's one-time champion boxer George Francombe. He fought 93 professional matches at welterweight winning 42, losing 37 and drawing 14. George fought Nobby Baker for the Welsh title unfortunately narrowly losing on points.

Acknowledgements

The author is indebted to numerous people and organisations for their help and advice during the production of this book. Their names are acknowledged below and sincere apologies are extended to anyone who may have been inadvertently omitted.

The Webb Family: Mrs Merle Stanning (daughter of Kenneth and Anita Webb), Michael and Richard (sons of Leslie and Emma Muriel Webb), John Martin (son of Martin and Elizabeth Webb), George Delme Murray (grandson of Tom Alexander and Emily Webb), Mrs Mary Southall (granddaughter of John Edgar and Margaret Annie Webb).

Friends and Colleagues: Brian Berrows, Brian Blake, Steve Burbage, Mrs Collings (ex Hanbury Hotel), Trevor and Ada Creed (ex Central Hotel), Pam Davies, Fred Griffiths, Len Head, Gary and Gill Higgins, Bill Hughes (ex Clynmawr), Cyril Jones, Dilwyn Jones, Arthur Kimber, Gwen Lewis, Victor Pettet, Kath Pritchard (nee Martindale), Don Probert, Eldred Probert, Graham Pullinge, Mrs Thompson (Fleet, Hants), Norman Walters, Mrs Warefield, Dolly Williams (ex Mitre Inn), Mary Williams.

Staff of the following concerns: Record Office Cwmbran, Reference Libraries at Cardiff, Newport and Treorchy. Old Bakehouse Publications Abertillery.

Special thanks to Mr Eric Thomas for his photographic expertise.

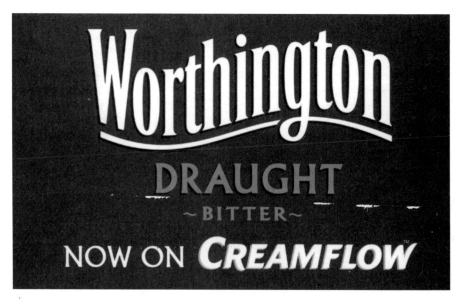